CALGARY PUBLIC LIBRARY

JAN   2018

For Gwenaëlle, who has passed on to our children Daé and Tenzor her love for natural, simple, healthy, and good food.

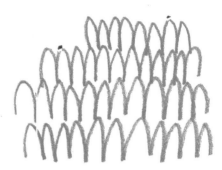

150 NEW RECIPES FOR
FRESH, HEALTHY DISHES

SIMPLE
NATURE

ALAIN DUCASSE

CHRISTOPHE SAINTAGNE
PAULE NEYRAT

RIZZOLI
NEW YORK

New York · Paris · London · Milan

Since 2009, when the first *Nature* cookbook came out, this word has come to mean much more to me than cuisine. For me, "Nature" is first of all a state of mind and way of thinking, an attitude toward life that is translated as genuinely as possible in my cuisine.

Now, six years on, I want to go even further. My conviction as a man and my commitment as a chef are strengthened and consolidated in this renewed concept of cuisine. At a time of great waste, industrial farming, and intensive agriculture and fishing, the need for a cuisine that is more oriented toward nature becomes more evident to me. Healthy, respectful, sincere, seasonal, concerned— "Nature" cuisine is summarized in the ten main principles stated in the introduction to this book. These are the principles that guide me daily and which I would like to share with you.

If we indeed are what we eat, then by eating better, we can only become better people.

With the assistance of my chef Christophe Saintagne and nutritionist Paule Neyrat, our concept has become embodied in 150 simple, healthy, and delicious dishes, the recipes for which come with practical tips for a cuisine that is sustainable and adapted to each season. This has nothing at all to do with diet. The key word is pleasure.

I would like to take the opportunity to thank my two Nature partners. Christophe has fulfilled his mission of transmitting our message through his talent and fabulous recipes. Paule has worked resolutely and cheerfully to ensure that the dishes are both balanced and simple.

They have helped me to make this book I had intended: A book that is about cooking, naturally, but mainly one that is filled with life and emotion.

ALAIN DUCASSE

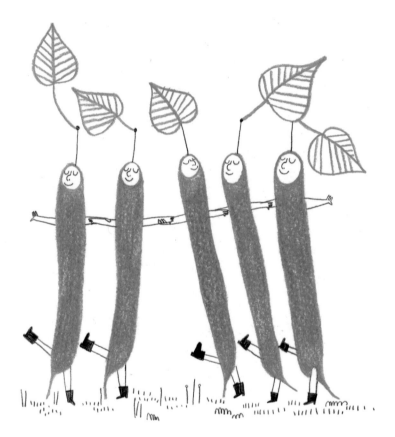

TABLE OF CONTENTS

● TOMATOES ALL YEAR-ROUND?

Alain Ducasse – The ones I find in winter have absolutely no flavor; nothing but water. They're grown out of the sun, in overheated greenhouses. A total waste of energy!

Paule Neyrat – Tomatoes are in season between June and September. This is the period when they are good, full of flavor and vitamins.

● BELL PEPPERS AND ZUCCHINI TOO?

AD – The same goes for them. They're also found year-round, but they're summer vegetables. They're imported or they're grown under glass, seeing as there is little sun in January.

PN – Ratatouille is a summer dish. It's made using vegetables that grow on plants with roots in the soil and heads in the sun.

● AND STRAWBERRIES?

AD – They're all tasteless out of season. Geneticists have invented a very tough strawberry: They can be knocked about; they don't complain; they stay firm and very red. They're easily shipped in refrigerated trucks or planes from the thousands of acres of plastic tunnels where they're grown on an industrial scale. Not in the earth, obviously, and out of the sun.

PN – Fresh strawberries can be found in markets between May and August. They are grown in fields and taste and smell like strawberries.

● WHY SHOULDN'T THEY BE EATEN OUT OF SEASON?

AD – First, because it's a terrible waste of energy that produces tons of CO_2 and contributes to the destruction of the planet!

PN – And because this doesn't serve our physiological needs. These vegetables have a particularly high water content, which we need in summer when it's hot and when we become dehydrated more easily, not in winter. They are also high in carotenes, which protect us against the damage caused by the summer sun. Mother nature has it all worked out.

Try to get close to nature and respect its (SEASON).

THE
FA
RM
ER'
S
MA
RK
ET

● WHY A FARMERS' MARKET?

AD - Because you do physical exercise, and it's good for your health. You can take a wheeled shopping bag if it hurts your back to carry a shopping basket

PN - But mainly because you have direct contact with the produce and producers. It's much more enjoyable than looking at a supermarket shelf or a self-checkout kiosk, don't you think?

● HOW OFTEN SHOULD YOU GO TO THE MARKET?

AD - As often as possible, but of course this depends on how you use your time. Once a week is a good start. There are farmers' markets everywhere on the weekend.

PN - Then you can stock up on vegetables that can keep for one week in the fridge. You can also buy more delicate fruits and vegetables that have to be eaten quickly.

● WHY A BASKET OR WHEELED SHOPPING BAG?

AD - Because a plastic bag needs 450 years to break down! You have to think before throwing things away in the country, and the same goes for the city.

PN - Reusable grocery bags are also good. I always keep a few in the car. Having them lets you say no to plastic bags in small shops. The fruits and vegetables are put inside paper bags and then arranged neatly inside the grocery bag. When you get home, you put the paper bags in the recycling bin.

THE TIME IT TAKES COMMON PRODUCTS TO BREAK DOWN

Paper : 2 to 5 month

Milk carton : 5 years

Chewing-gum : 5 years

Candy wrapper : 5 years

Steel can : 50 to 100 years

Aluminium can : 200 years

Plastic 6-pack ring : 400 years

Go to the market
and fill your basket.

ORGANIC FOOD

● WHY CHOOSE ORGANIC PRODUCE?

AD - Because the vegetables, fruits, and grains are grown without the use of synthetic chemicals. And animals are reared the traditional way, not on an industrial scale.

PN - This not only helps to save the planet, but also our health, because all of those chemical products are toxic and contain such things as antibiotics, which are found in the meat of animals.

● HOW CAN IT BE RECOGNIZED?

AD - Organically farmed produce carries a French or European organic certification label; in the United States, the USDA designates produce farmed per its organic standards. It's an official sign of quality, like PDO, PGI, or Label Rouge.

PN - It's strictly controlled and monitored, especially in France.

● DOES IT TASTE BETTER?

AD - More often it does. Fruits and vegetables are grown depending on the season, and livestock is fed on grass and grains. But if an organic fruit is picked before it's ripe, it won't taste good.

PN - When it's at its peak ripeness, fresh organic produce is better because it contains less water than that grown on an industrial scale, which concentrates its flavors.

● AND ON THE POCKET?

AD - When you buy directly from a small-scale producer, it's less expensive.

PN - There are quite a few who have formed associations. They sell their produce online and deliver to your home. You can also subscribe to a CSA, which allows you to pick up seasonal organic produce every week.

BUY ORGANIC PRODUCE
WHENEVER you CAN find it.

● WHAT'S A SHORT FOOD-SUPPLY CHAIN?

AD - It's a supply chain with only one intermediary at most between the producer and the consumer.

PN - It's when you buy your vegetables from a farmers' market and not from a wholesale market. Or from an association that is supplied directly by small-scale producers. Or directly from a producer, either online or straight from the farm.

● WHAT'S THE ADVANTAGE OF THAT?

AD - Generally speaking, it tends to be cheaper because there aren't thirty-six intermediaries taking a cut each time. As a result, the producers are better paid.

PN - There's also less waste! The produce is fresher and better quality.

AD - And you know where it comes from, which is the nicest thing. Ideally, it's when you can buy fruits and vegetables that are locally grown in the region, within a radius of 250 kilometers (150 miles).

● SO IF YOU LIVE IN NEW YORK STATE, YOU CAN'T EAT AVOCADOS? IS THAT IT?

AD - Of course not! We're talking about everyday fruits and vegetable — leeks, carrots, potatoes, apples, pears — which grow in most regions. Otherwise, you'd never eat a banana and many people would never eat an orange!

● IS FAIR TRADE THE SAME THING?

AD - That refers to producers in the poorer countries of the world: They are better paid with fair trade, and they aren't exploited by the international brands that make huge profits.

PN - Those producers also use environmentally friendly farming methods. They're often organic.

AD - If you buy fair trade quinoa from Bolivia, for instance, you can be sure that the farmers are better paid. A lot of fair trade products are available now, so you should choose them.

SUSTAINABLE FISHING

● WHAT IS SUSTAINABLE FISHING?

AD - It's also known as responsible fishing. Every sea and ocean is becoming increasingly depopulated as the result of intensive fishing and the use of methods that hinder fish from reproducing.

PN - Certain fish species shouldn't be caught anymore, like bluefin tuna, for example, which is heading for extinction. Others should only be captured in seas where they are still abundant or at certain times and in certain quantities.

● HOW IS IT ALL MONITORED?

AD - FAO, The Food and Agriculture Organization of the United Nations, has set out a code of conduct for responsible fisheries with the aim of preserving marine resources. The European Union has set up a quota system.

PN - Different international organizations are also used to monitor and denounce overfishing. A label has been created by the MSC, the Marine Stewardship Council, to guarantee that the fish you eat is a product of responsible fishing.

● WHAT IF YOU ONLY LIKE SOLE?

AD - You can eat it from time to time if it was caught in the North Sea or the Bay of Biscay. But if it's sole from Senegal, you shouldn't buy it because the sole found along the African coast is endangered.

PN - Look at the label, on the fishmonger's stall: It is mandatory to indicate the place where it was caught.

● HOW CAN YOU KNOW WHETHER A FISH IS ENDANGERED OR NOT?

AD - Search the Greenpeace, WWF, or Mr. Goodfish websites: Their lists are updated regularly.

EAT fish,
AND support sustainable fishing.

LE
SS
ME
AT

🔹 SHOULD YOU BECOME A VEGETARIAN?

AD - No, not really. But the intensive rearing of animals for meat is a catastrophe for the planet.

PN - And too much red meat is not the best thing for your health. An overwhelming number of scientific studies prove it.

🔹 SO, WHAT SHOULD YOU DO?

AD - Always choose meat and poultry from small-scale producers who rear their animals well. The meat will be much better; there's no comparison.

PN - You should only eat between 300 and 500 grams (10 1/2 ounces—1 pound 2 ounces) a week at the most. That's more than enough. Per week, not per day! There's nothing to stop you enjoying a big rib steak and then not eating meat the next day.

🔹 IF THERE'S NO MEAT IN A MEAL, YOU OFTEN GET THE FEELING OF NOT HAVING EATEN.

AD - That's because meals aren't properly balanced. If you ate more vegetables and grains, you wouldn't have this impression.

PN - Their high dietary fiber carbohydrate content make you feel full. If you start dinner with a hearty vegetable soup, you practically won't feel hungry afterward. It's the same when you eat pasta or risotto.

🔹 BUT WON'T YOU MISS OUT ON PROTEIN?

AD - You'll find it in fish, eggs, and dairy products.

PN - That's for animal proteins; it isn't a reason to stuff yourself. Grains and dried and fresh legumes give you plant protein. That's how you get the balance.

CONSUME less meat, AND favor VEGETABLE produce.

THE SECRET OF BEING SLIM

...IS HAVING A BALANCED DIET!

PN - Exactly. When you eat a little of everything, you balance your diet without going to a whole lot of trouble. You have a kind of app in your brain that controls everything you eat, depending on your energy requirements.

AD - So you should listen to it. Only eat when you actually feel hungry. And, more important, stop when you feel full.

● WHAT IF YOU ALWAYS FEEL HUNGRY?

PN - Then it's because you eat too fast, without thinking about what you're eating, without savoring it.

AD - Quite simply, take the time to savor a piece of good bread at the start of a meal. That will turn on the "hungry/full" app.

PN - It records everything you swallow, the calories, protein, carbohydrate, and so forth. And it progressively sends signals; you feel less and less hungry. And when you're full, you spontaneously stop eating.

AD - But you have to chew properly; otherwise, it won't work.

● SO IT'S ACTUALLY AN BUILT-IN CALORIE COUNTER?

PN - Exactly! So you don't have to go to great lengths to count the calories in food. That's a waste of time.

AD - It's important to take the time to sit at the table, to have a proper meal, and not to snack on anything at any time.

● WHAT DO YOU MEAN BY A PROPER MEAL?

AD - - An one-dish meal, comprising vegetable and/or grains, possibly a little animal protein (meat, fish, or egg), some dairy or cheese, and a fruit, all accompanied by a good bread.

PN - But you can be flexible; you can also start with a good soup, continue with a fish or chicken, or pasta. It can be varied every day. The main thing is to eat a bit of everything and to eat slowly. This is essential if you're to taste the products and distinguish the different flavors. You have to enjoy them. It's what I do when I try a dish.

By EATING slowLy,
AND A Bit of everything,
you will STAY slim.

SHOULD YOU DIET?

AD – Given the obesity epidemic throughout our world, you have to be on your guard.

PN – It's true that too much fat and too much sugar upset the dietary balance. When you snack on fatty and sugary products, when you drink soda throughout the day, you no longer feel like eating vegetables.

AD – – It messes with all your sensations; it blurs all the markers that tell you whether you're hungry or sated.

BUT SALT ISN'T FATTENING, IS IT?

PN – It isn't directly fattening, because it contains no calories. But it stimulates the appetite, which often makes you eat more or snack on very salty foods like potato chips. It isn't just a matter of weight.

WHAT IS IT A QUESTION OF, THEN?

PN – It's a matter of health in general. Eating too much fat, too much salt, and too much sugar isn't at all good for your body. It ends up clogging your arteries, and that isn't at all good for your heart.

AD – It's also a matter of preserving flavors; you have to be careful not to spoil products by cooking them. If you add too much fat, they become denatured.

BUT ISN'T SALT A FLAVOR ENHANCER?

AD – Yes, but only in the right proportion. The same goes for sugar: When there's too much in a dessert, the taste buds become overwhelmed and the flavors of the ingredients can no longer be perceived.

Try to go _EASY_ on fat, sugar, and salt in your cooking.

● COOKING SIMPLY ALSO MEANS BEING WELL ORGANIZED.

AD - You have to think ahead; you have to prep food like professionals do. You peel, wash, and cut up all the vegetables at the same time.

PN - An oven takes 10 to 15 minutes to heat up. Turn it on ahead of time, not at the last minute.

AD - A basic rule is to start by cooking the things that take the longest, even if it's the dessert. While it's cooking and cooling, you can take care of the rest. When you're making a tart crust, double the amount of pastry you make and freeze the other half. The same goes for a vegetable soup, which can be made to last several days.

● SHOULD TIME-SAVING EQUIPMENT BE USED?

AD - For certain things, why not? But not for everything. A pesto is always better when pounded in a mortar rather than chopped up in a blender. If you don't have one, you can use a bowl and a small pestle.

PN - And besides, you can give the muscles in your arms a good workout.

AD - Actually, you can cook practically everything with a saucepan, a frying pan, a cast-iron Dutch oven, an oven, two knives (one small and one large), and a handheld immersion blender.

● GREAT IDEAS FOR PEOPLE IN A HURRY.

AD - It isn't just a matter of time, but of showing respect for your ingredients. The more simply you cook, the more you show respect for foods and their flavors. That's essential!

PN - And you also save time. For instance, when you cook vegetables and keep them crunchy you're keeping their vitamins intact.

☛ IS IT JUST FASHIONABLE TO TALK ABOUT FOOD WASTE ?

AD - It isn't about fashion, it's a real problem. Waste just isn't possible. The French are estimated to throw away 20 to 30 kilograms (44 to 66 pounds) of food per person each year, 7 kilograms (15 1/2 pounds) of which is still intact, not even unwrapped!

PN - And yet it can't be difficult to throw away as little as possible.

☛ HOW CAN WE DO THIS ?

PN - First, you have to buy less; that way you won't risk having to throw away shriveled-up vegetables or food that's past its use-by date.

AD - You should write a shopping list, thinking about what you still have in the fridge or in your cupboards.

PN - And before buying groceries, you should work out the meals you want to make during the week.

☛ AND LEFTOVERS ?

AD - The leftovers from cooked meals can be put in a container and stored in the refrigerator or freezer.

PN - With a label telling you what's inside and the date.

AD - This is essential, otherwise it might end up forgotten at the back of the fridge.

PN - I actually have a small vacuum sealer for storing food in bags or containers. It's very practical, because everything keeps for a long time. No food ever gets thrown away.

THROW AWAY AS little AS possible,
AND RE-USE leftovers.

BLACK RADISHES

CABBAGE

CARROTS

CAULIFLOWER

CELERY ROOT

CHARD

CHESTNUTS

ENDIVE

GREENS

LEEKS

MUSHROOMS

PARSNIPS

POTATOES

SPINACH

SQUASH

SWISS CHARD

TURNIPS

WATERCRESS

APPLES

BLACKBERRIES

GRAPES

HAZELNUTS

KIWI

NUTS

ORANGE

PEARS

PINEAPPLE

FALL

CREAM OF CELERY AND GORGONZOLA

SERVES 4
PREPARATION TIME: 10 MINUTES
COOK TIME: 30 MINUTES

1 celeriac, about 900 grams - 2 pounds
2 medium potatoes
1 bunch chives
1 liter - 4 1/4 cups chicken broth (see p. 42)
100 grams - 3 1/2 ounces Gorgonzola cheese
1 rounded tablespoon (25 grams - 1 ounces) mascarpone cheese
2 tablespoons olive oil
2 tablespoons red wine vinegar
Salt
Freshly ground pepper

Prepare the vegetables
Peel, wash, and quarter the celeriac. Cut three of the pieces into a small dice and the fourth into thin strips. Set aside separately in two bowls. Peel, wash, and dice the potatoes. Add to the bowl with the diced celeriac. Rinse, dry, and finely chop the chives. Add them to the celeriac strips.

Make the celery cream
Put the diced celeriac and potato into a saucepan. Add the chicken broth and cook over medium heat until the celeriac is quite soft (a knife should slide in easily), about 25 minutes. Use a handheld immersion blender to blend until very smooth.

Finish and serve
Add the Gorgonzola and mascarpone to the pan with the blended celeriac and potato soup. Simmer until the cheese has melted, stirring from time to time. If the soup is too thick, dilute it with a little chicken broth. Blend briefly with the handheld blender. Season with salt and pepper.

Add the olive oil and vinegar to the bowl with the celeriac strips and chives, and season with salt and pepper. Mix well. Serve the vegetables on four heated soup plates. Transfer the cream of celery soup to a tureen and serve at the table on the soup plates.

AD - This soup has a strong but well-balanced flavor. The sweetness of the mascarpone tones down the celeriac and Gorgonzola.

PN - I really like this because it contains calcium from the cheese.

CHESTNUT AND ROSEMARY CONDIMENT

SERVES 4

PREPARATION TIME: 5 MINUTES

COOK TIME: 30 MINUTES

REST TIME: 10 MINUTES

2 shallots
200 milliliters - 3/4 cup
plus 1 tablespoon olive oil
250 grams - 9 ounces cooked
chestnuts (from a jar or
vacuum-packed), divided
1 cup lowfat (2%) milk
Salt
Freshly ground pepper
4 sprigs rosemary

Make the condiment

Peel and chop the shallots. Heat 1 tablespoon of the olive oil in a small saucepan over low heat and cook the shallots until they are browned and soft. Add 200 grams - 7 ounces of the chestnuts to the shallots, moisten with the milk, and stir. Season with salt and pepper, and simmer until the chestnuts are tender. Chop the remaining chestnuts and set aside.

Remove from the heat. Add the rosemary sprigs, cover with a lid, and infuse for 10 minutes.

Finish

Remove the rosemary sprigs. Transfer the contents of the pan to the jar of a blender and blend, gradually adding the remaining olive oil, until smooth. Transfer to a bowl and add the remaining chestnuts. Let cool, then cover the bowl with plastic wrap (cling film) and refrigerate. You can keep it 3 to 4 days in the fridge.

Serve

Before serving, reheat the condiment a little while stirring. Serve warm.

AD - Chestnut and rosemary are an unexpected combination, but it works very well. The slight acidity of the shallots enhances the sweetness of the chestnuts. This condiment is very refined.

PN - I hope moms use this to spread on bread for their children. It's a good way to train their taste buds.

33

ROASTED PARSNIPS WITH HONEY AND MINT

SERVES 4
PREPARATION TIME: 5 MINUTES
COOK TIME: 20 MINUTES

12 small, young parsnips
1 tablespoon olive oil
Juice of 1 lemon
Salt
2 tablespoons honey,
preferably fir honeydew
4 tablespoons red wine
vinegar
300 milliliters - 1/3 cup
plus 4 tablespoons poule au
pot (chicken) broth
(see p. 62)
3 juniper berries
2 sprigs mint

Prepare the parsnips

Peel and wash the parsnips. Halve them lengthwise if they are thick; if not, leave them whole. Immerse them as you work in a bowl of water with the lemon juice.

Cook the parsnips

Heat the olive oil in a cast-iron pan with lid. Drain and dry the parsnips, transfer them to the pan, and season with salt. Cook for 5 minutes, stirring, until they turn a golden brown.

Add the honey and stir. Cook for 5 minutes until the parsnips are well colored.

Deglaze with the vinegar and scrape the pan well to recover all the caramelized bits. Add the chicken broth. Stir. Chop the juniper berries and add them to the pan. Stir again and cover the pan. Cook for 6–8 minutes. Check that the parsnips are soft using the tip of a knife; it should slide in easily.

Finish and serve

Rinse, dry, and pluck the mint leaves. Remove the pan from the heat. Add the mint leaves and stir.

Use a slotted spoon to transfer the parsnips to a platter or individual plates. Taste the cooking liquid and adjust the seasoning with salt, if necessary. Mix well and pour over the parsnips. Serve immediately.

AD - A sweet and savory appetizer brought to life by Christophe Saintagne's creativity. I was in for a real treat when he asked me to try these parsnips. This recipe can also be made with carrots. Why not? I'll have to try it.

PN - Until the Renaissance, people didn't differentiate between carrots and parsnips. At the time, carrots were as white as parsnips and not yet orange.

CREAM OF WATERCRESS WITH SOFT-BOILED EGGS

SERVES 4
PREPARATION TIME: 15 MINUTES
COOK TIME: 30 MINUTES

4 bunches watercress
1/2 white onion
2 medium potatoes
Olive oil
750 milliliters - 3 cups
poule au pot (chicken) broth
(see p. 62)
50 grams - 2 ounces smoked
bacon
Red wine Vinegar
4 eggs
100 milliliters - 1/3 cup
plus 1 tablespoon lowfat (2%)
milk
100 milliliters - 1/3 cup
plus 1 tablespoon light cream
Salt
Freshly ground pepper

AD - Peeling soft-boiled eggs is always fraught with danger. When you take them out of the water, tap them to break the shell a little and immerse them in lukewarm water (not hot, otherwise they will continue to cook). The water will penetrate the shell and make peeling easier.

PN - There's no need for meat or fish with this meal; an egg is enough. That said, watercress is a miracle food because it's high in iron, folic acid, and vitamin C, which is an excellent combination for increasing red blood cell production.

Make the watercress cream
Wash the watercress. Set aside 10 sprigs. Pluck the leaves from the remaining sprigs and set aside. Coarsely chop the stems. Peel and finely chop the onion. Peel and wash the potatoes and finely dice.

Heat a little olive oil in a saucepan. Brown the chopped watercress stems and the onion for 2–3 minutes. Add the diced potatoes and moisten with the chicken broth. Simmer for 15 minutes.

Prepare the soft-boiled eggs and the bacon
Cut the bacon into small strips. Heat a little olive oil in a frying pan and brown the bacon until crispy. Transfer to paper towels. Keep warm.

Heat 1 L – 4 1/2 cups water with a splash of vinegar in a saucepan and bring to a boil. Carefully add the eggs, then cook, uncovered, for 5 minutes.

Finish the watercress cream
Add the watercress leaves, milk, and cream to the potato mixture. Mix and cook for 2–3 minutes. Remove the saucepan from the heat. Blend until perfectly smooth with a handheld immersion blender. Season with salt and pepper.

Serve
Peel the eggs. Pluck the leaves from the reserved watercress sprigs. Serve the watercress cream on soup plates. Scatter the bacon and watercress leaves over the top. Place 1 egg on each soup plate and make a small cut into the yolk with a knife. Season with a turn of the pepper mill and serve immediately.

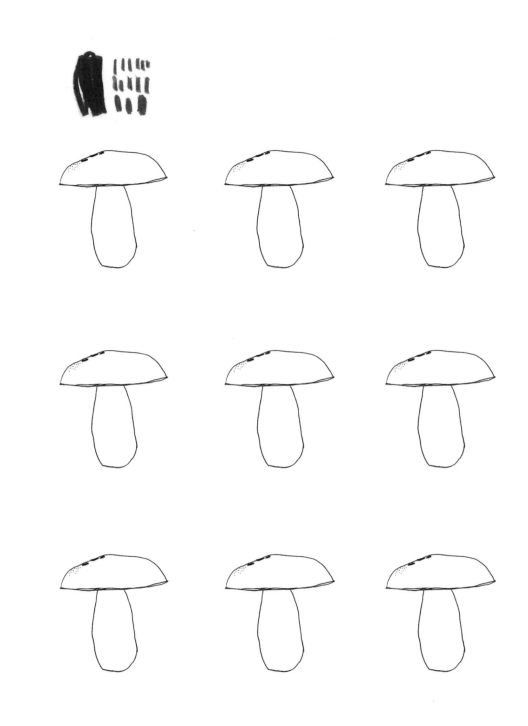

MUSHROOM BROTH

SERVES 4
PREPARATION TIME: 10 MINUTES
COOK TIME: 20 MINUTES

1.5 liters - 6 1/3 cups
poule au pot (chicken) or
pot-au-feu broth (pp. 62 and
150)
40 grams - 1 1/2 ounces
dried morels or other dried
mushrooms
150 grams - 5 1/2 ounces
white mushrooms
Leftover vegetables from
making poule au pot (p. 62)
or pot-au-feu (p. 150)
1/4 horseradish root, about
50 grams - 2 ounces
4 handfuls vermicelli
1 tablespoon soy sauce
Salt
Freshly ground pepper
Grated Comté cheese

Make the morel broth
Remove the layer of fat solidified on the top of the cold pot-au-feu or poule au pot broth; reserve the fat for another use. Transfer the broth to a saucepan and heat.

Chop the dried mushrooms. Put in a strainer and rinse under warm running water. Add them to the hot broth. Remove the pan from the heat and infuse for 15 minutes.

Prepare the vegetables
Meanwhile, cut the earthy stems off the white mushrooms and discard. Wash, dry, and cut the mushroom tops into a small dice. Likewise, dice the leftover poule au pot or pot-au-feu vegetables. Peel, wash, and grate the horseradish.

Finish the soup
Return the pan to the heat and bring to a boil. Then add the noodles. Stir and cook for 2–3 minutes. Add the white mushrooms, vegetables, and horseradish, and mix well. Season with the soy sauce. Check and adjust the seasoning with salt and pepper.

Transfer the mushroom broth to a tureen and serve in bowls. Pass the grated cheese separately.

AD - This is a good way to use the leftovers from a pot-au-feu or poule au pot. The flavor of the broth will change depending on the dried mushrooms you choose. It has a more rustic flavor with porcini mushrooms and a more sophisticated flavor with morels.

PN - This soup is amazing. The noodles provide carbohydrates; the vegetables provide dietary fiber and minerals; and the cheese provides calcium. I love it.

COLD VELOUTÉ OF BLACK RADISH WITH BUTTERMILK AND HORSERADISH

SERVES 4
PREPARATION TIME: 10 MINUTES
COOK TIME: 35 MINUTES

3 black radishes
3 medium size potatoes,
preferably Agria
10 grams - 2 teaspoons butter
Olive oil
500 milliliters - 2 cups *lait
ribot* or buttermilk
1/4 horseradish root, about
50 grams - 2 ounces
Salt

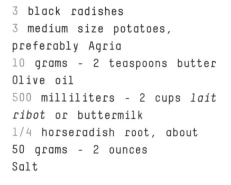

Prepare the black radishes
Wash the radishes well. Peel 2 of them and leave the third with the skin on. Finely dice all of them. Reserve 4 tablespoons of diced radish in a bowl.

Prepare the potatoes
Peel and wash the potatoes. Cut 2 of them into very thin rounds and the third into a small dice. Set them aside separately.

Make the velouté
Heat the butter and a little olive oil in a saucepan. Cook all but the reserved 4 tablespoons diced radish until browned, about 2 minutes. Add the potato rounds, lait ribot, and 500 milliliters - 2 cups water. Stir and cook for 30 minutes.

Prepare a bowl with a lot of ice and a little water. Off the heat, use a handheld immersion blender to blend the velouté until very smooth. Immediately transfer to a bowl and place it over the bowl filled with ice. Mix the velouté to cool it, then refrigerate for at least 20 minutes until it's cold.

Finish and serve
Heat 1 tablespoon olive oil in a cast-iron pan. Add the reserved diced radish and potato. Sweat for 4 minutes while stirring. Peel and grate the horseradish and add it to the pan. Mix.

Serve the vegetables on four heated soup plates. Transfer the very cold velouté to a tureen and serve at the table on the soup plates.

AD - Buttermilk is like lait ribot from Brittany; it's the liquid that's left when butter is churned. It's Christophe Saintagne's pet ingredient, and I also like it a lot. It adds a very subtle touch of sourness.

PN - And as for black radish, it's the darling of detox lovers. Its juice is commonly used in phytotherapy to treat digestive problems. This velouté will go down very easily.

SALT COD WITH SWISS CHARD AND GRAPES

400 grams - 14 ounces salt cod
750 milliliters - 3 cups
lowfat (2%) milk
1 onion
1 bunch young Swiss chard
1 bunch black grapes
1 bunch white grapes
Olive oil
100 milliliters - 1/3 cup
plus 1 tablespoon poule au pot
(chicken) broth (see p. 62)
1 clove garlic
Salt
Freshly ground pepper

AD - To know whether the cod is properly desalted, you have to taste it several times while desalting. Three hours is the average time, depending on the intensity of the salting process.

PN - This is the ideal one-dish meal. It has everything, but without the fat. With a small serving of soup or salad to start, a yogurt, and a piece of fruit, you have a very special low-cal meal.

Prepare the salt cod
Put the cod in a container and cover with plenty of water. Soak for 2-3 hours, changing the water several times. Transfer to paper towels and dry.

Put the milk into a saucepan and add the cod. Heat the milk to a gentle boil and simmer for 3-4 minutes. Transfer the fish to a dish and keep it warm.

Prepare the chard, onion, and grapes
Peel and finely chop the onion. Wash the chard and separate the stems from the leaves. Peel and quarter each stem. Wash both bunches of grapes, then separate into individual grapes.

Cook the chard stems
Heat a little olive oil in a cast-iron pan. Add the chopped onions and brown well. Add the chard stems and sweat for 3 minutes. Add the

chicken broth and cook over medium heat for 12 minutes. Add the grapes, stir, and cook for 2 minutes more.

Cook the chard leaves
In the meantime, stack the chard leaves, roll them up, and coarsely chop. Peel the garlic clove. Prick the clove with a fork and leave it on the end.

Heat a little olive oil in a frying pan, add the chopped chard leaves, and stir with the garlic clove on the end of the fork. Cook the leaves until they wilt. Season with salt and pepper.

Finish
Arrange the chard stems and grapes on a serving dish and surround with chard leaves. Flake the cod and place on top. Sprinkle generously with freshly ground pepper and serve.

POULE AU POT BROTH WITH UDON

SERVES 4
PREPARATION TIME: 15 MINUTES
COOKING TIME: 15 MINUTES

1 liter - 4 1/4 cups poule
au pot (chicken) broth
(see p. 62)
4 stalks celery
2 carrots
4 turnips
1 leek
4 large white mushrooms
2 onions
Salt
2 tablespoons miso paste
200 grams - 7 ounces
udon noodles
Freshly ground pepper

AD - Udon noodles are soft noodles made from wheat, which are very popular in Japan. They're quite thick (1.7-3.8 millimeters - 1/16-1/8-inch) but cook quickly. They can be found at Asian grocery stores and online.

PN - This is a tasty soup filled with good carbs, dietary fiber, and minerals, and which you have to chew. It fills you up at the start of the meal, so you eat less afterward. That's one of the secrets to staying slim. Thank you, chef!

Defat the broth
Remove the layer of fat solidified on the top of the cold broth. Put 2 tablespoons of this fat in a cast-iron pot with lid or Dutch oven.

Prepare the vegetables
Wash and peel the carrots and turnips; remove the tough strings from the celery. Cut off the tough green tops of the leek. Trim the mushroom stems. Peel the onions. Chop the vegetables into small pieces.

Prepare the broth
Heat the pot with the chicken fat, then add the chopped vegetables and season well with salt. Cover with a lid and braise for 5 minutes. Add the broth and miso paste, and bring to a boil. Skim off the foam that floats to the surface, then add the noodles and cook for about 10 minutes.

Finish and serve
Heat four bowls. Pass the contents of the pan through a strainer into a saucepan. Place over medium heat. Divide the noodles and vegetables and serve on warmed soup plates.

Adjust the seasoning of the broth with salt and pepper, check that it is at the correct temperature, and transfer to a pitcher. Serve at the table, pouring the broth over the noodles and vegetables.

DUCK WITH BLACK TURNIP AND PEAR

SERVES 4-6
PREPARATION TIME: 15 MINUTES
COOK TIME: 50 MINUTES

1 white onion
8 black turnips (or generic turnip)
1 oven-ready duckling, about 1.2 kilograms - 2 pounds 12 ounces
Olive oil
Duck fat
1 teaspoon honey
5 coriander seeds
Salt
Freshly ground pepper
300 milliliters - 1/3 cup plus 4 tablespoons chicken broth
3 large pears
1 bunch cilantro (coriander)

Prepare the vegetables
Peel and finely chop the onion. Peel and wash the turnips. Quarter them and set aside.

Cook the duckling
Add a little olive oil to a cast-iron pan and heat on high heat. Brown the duckling on all sides. Transfer the duckling to a plate and discard the oil from the pan. Put 1 tablespoon duck fat in the pan and sweat the chopped onion for 5 minutes. Then return the duckling to the pan and add the turnips, honey, and coriander seeds. Sir and season with salt and pepper. Add the chicken broth. Cook for 40 minutes, turning the duckling over several times.

Prepare the pears
In the meantime, wash the pears. Quarter them and remove the seeds. Melt one tablespoon duck fat in a frying pan. Brown the pears on all sides for 2-3 minutes, while basting with the fat.

Finish
Rinse, dry, pluck, and chop the cilantro leaves. Transfer the duckling to a serving dish. Remove the turnips with a slotted spoon and arrange them around the duckling, alternating them with the pear quarters. Scatter the chopped cilantro leaves over the top.

Reduce the cooking liquid over high heat until it has thickened slightly. Serve separately in a sauce boat.

SMOKED HERRING-STUFFED CABBAGE

300 grams - 10 1/2 ounces lightly smoked whole herrings (bloaters)
500 milliliters - 2 cups lowfat (2%) milk
Salt
1 head Savoy cabbage, about 700 grams - 1 pound 9 ounces
10 grams - 2 teaspoons butter
300 grams - 10 1/2 ounces potatoes, preferably Agria
2 carrots
1 onion

4 stalks celery
1/2 bunch flat-leaf parsley
1/2 bunch tarragon
2 egg yolks
40 grams - 1 1/2 ounces/3/8 cup grated Parmesan cheese
4 grams juniper berry powder
Freshly ground pepper
Olive oil
50 milliliters - 3 1/2 tablespoons white wine
250 milliliters - 1 cup chicken broth

Soak the herring

In a bowl, soak the fish in the milk for 2 hours to remove the salt. Drain the fish, skin it, and cut the flesh into thin slices. Transfer to a clean bowl. Discard the milk.

Prepare the cabbage

Bring a saucepan of salted water to a boil and prepare a bowl with water and ice cubes. Remove 8–10 outer leaves from the cabbage. Immerse them in the boiling water for 2 minutes. Transfer them to the ice water. Remove from the ice water and cut off the bottom of the central rib. Set aside these blanched leaves. Thinly slice the core of the cabbage. Blanch and shock the slices in the same way as the leaves, and then drain. Reserve the saucepan with salted water.

Melt the butter in a sauté pan and sweat the cabbage slices for 5 minutes. Season lightly with salt and set aside.

Make the mashed potatoes

Wash the unpeeled potatoes. Bring the saucepan with salted water to a boil and cook the potatoes until tender, about 20 minutes depending on their size. When tender, they should be easily pierced with a knife. Let cool slightly, then peel them and mash with a fork. Peel and finely dice the carrots, onion, and celery.

Make the stuffing

Rinse, pluck, and chop the parsley and tarragon leaves. Add to the bowl with the fish, and then add the mashed potato, egg yolks, Parmesan, and juniper berry powder. Mix. Adjust the seasoning with salt and pepper. Prepare the stuffed cabbage and vegetable garnish, then serve

Preheat the oven to 180°C - 350°F (gas mark 4). Divide the stuffing into four equal portions. Overlap 2 blanched cabbage leaves and place one portion of stuffing on top. Fold the leaves over to form a ball. Hold it in place by tying with kitchen twine. Make another 3 stuffed cabbage balls. In a sauté pan or ovenproof dish, heat a little olive oil and sweat the diced vegetables for 2–3 minutes. Deglaze the pan with the white wine, put in the 4 stuffed cabbage balls, add the chicken broth, and bake for 15–20 minutes.

Remove from the oven and serve one cabbage ball and the vegetables on each plate.

VELOUTÉ OF CHESTNUT AND HARE

SERVES 4
PREPARATION TIME: 30 MINUTES + MARINATING TIME
COOK TIME: 1 HOUR 30 MINUTES
REST TIME: 12 HOURS

2 hare forequarters
2 carrots
2 white onions
2 cloves garlic
3 juniper berries
2 sprigs thyme
2 sprigs rosemary
1 liter - 4 1/4 cups red wine
100 milliliters - 1/3 cup plus 1 tablespoon cognac
Freshly ground pepper
Olive oil
Salt
300 grams - 10 1/2 ounces cooked chestnuts (from a jar or vacuum-packed)
200 milliliters - 3/4 cup plus 1 tablespoon light cream
2 pinches juniper berry powder
2 sprigs flat-leaf parsley

Prepare the hare a day ahead
Put the hare forequarters in a large bowl. Peel and slice the carrots. Peel and finely slice the onions. Add the vegetables to the bowl, and then add the crushed garlic cloves, juniper berries, thyme, and rosemary. Add the wine and cognac, and season generously with pepper. Marinate for 12 hours in the refrigerator.

Cook the hare
Preheat the oven to 150°C - 300°F (gas mark 2). Add a little olive oil to a cast-iron pot or Dutch oven on high heat. Remove the hare from the marinade, pat dry, season with salt, and brown on all sides. Transfer to a plate.

Pass the marinade through a strainer into a bowl. Put the vegetables from the marinade in the pot and brown for 2-3 minutes. Return the hare to the pot and add the marinade. Bring it to a boil and skim off the foam. Cover with a lid and bake in the oven for 1 hour 15 minutes. Check that the hare is cooked through and remove the garlic cloves, juniper berries, thyme, and rosemary.

Make the velouté
Shred the hare, then return the meat to the pot. Set aside a few chestnuts and add the rest to the pot together with the cream. Cook for 5 minutes, and then blend until smooth with a handheld immersion blender. Keep warm.

Serve
Rinse, dry, and pluck the parsley leaves. Check and adjust the velouté seasoning and add the juniper berry powder. Serve the velouté in a tureen or in bowls. Add the reserved chestnuts and parsley leaves to the bowls. Serve very hot.

SQUASH

There are so many varieties of squash throughout the world that one really can't speak of this vegetable, which belongs to the vast *Cucurbitaceae* family, in the singular. Their common characteristic is their thick and tough skin, which ranges in color among orange, green, yellow, and white, protecting a juicy flesh that contains many seeds. They vary greatly in weight, ranging between a few hundred grams (less than ten ounces) and ten kilograms (twenty-two pounds), and shape, growing round, oval, elongated, and bent. Squashes date back to the dawn of time (150,000 years before the present era). Birds spread their seeds all over the planet. It was for their highly nourishing seeds that squashes were first cultivated, because the little flesh they had was often bitter. Dried squashes were turned into containers, musical instruments, and religious objects.

● VARIETIES AND SEASONS

Squashes grow throughout the year, and a distinction is made between winter squashes and summer squashes.

Winter squash : These are always harvested when ripe, and include the varieties *Cucurbita pepo* (also known as the summer squash) and *Cucurbita maxima* (also known as the winter squash), both commonly known as pumpkin and often confused; butternut squash, not to be confused with buttercup squash; Hubbard squash; turban squash; acorn squash, also known as pepper squash; delicata squash; spaghetti squash; and ambercup squash.

Summer squash : the most common is the zucchini, of which there are many varieties, among them elongated and relatively straight ones, and round ones. There are also the yellow crookneck, marrow, and pattypan squash varieties.

● CHOOSING AND STORAGE

The skin of winter squashes should be dull, a sign of ripeness, while the skin of a good summer squash should be quite shiny. Winter squashes can be stored for several weeks in a cold place (10-15°C/50-60°F) and away from light. They do not withstand refrigeration. However, summer squashes are suited to storing in the refrigerator..

● NUTRITION

Squashes have few calories, but contain large amounts of different protective antioxidants. The more orange their flesh, the more they have.

● USES AND COMBINATIONS

Squashes can always be prepared with very little water, and can be made into soups, gratin dishes, stuffings, tarts, cakes, and more. They combine well with both spices and sugar.

STUFFED BUTTERNUT SQUASH

1 butternut squash, about 1 kilogram - 2 pounds 4 ounces
500 grams - 2 pounds 3 ounces/2 1/4 cups coarse salt
Salt
150 grams - 5 1/2 ounces/ 1 cup bulgur
2 shallots
1/2 bunch flat-leaf parsley
300 grams - 10 1/2 ounces leftover meat from poule au pot (see p. 62) or pot-au-feu (see p. 150)
Olive oil
Freshly ground pepper
30 grams - 1/3 cup grated Parmesan cheese

AD - Butternut squash is a cultivar of the species Cucurbita moschata. It has a very sweet flavor, hence the "butter" in its name.

PN - Like all squashes, butternut squash contains large amounts of antioxidant carotenes and minerals. People who are gluten-free can replace the bulgur with quinoa

Cook the squash
Preheat the oven to 170°C - 340°F (gas mark 3-4). Wash and dry the squash. Cover a baking sheet with coarse salt, put the squash on the sheet, and cook in the oven for 1 hour. Turn it over and cook for 1 hour more. Transfer the squash to a plate and let it rest for 20 minutes. Set aside the baking sheet with the salt. Increase the oven temperature to 180°C - 350°F (gas mark 4).

Cook the bulgur wheat
In the meantime, put 500 milliliters - 2 cups water in a saucepan. Lightly salt and bring to a boil. Add the bulgur, mix, lower the heat, and let the bulgur absorb the water. Mix from time to time, then cover and let it rest.

Prepare the squash
Cut off the top of the cooked squash at about one quarter of its height. Remove and discard the seeds and strings from the squash. Then use a teaspoon to scoop out the flesh. Set aside the flesh and hollowed out squash.

Make the stuffing
Peel and chop the shallots. Rinse, dry, pluck, and chop the parsley leaves. Shred the leftover poule au pot or pot-au-feu meat. Heat a little olive oil in a frying pan and sweat the shallots without coloring them. Add the squash flesh and cook for 5 minutes while stirring. Season with salt and pepper. Transfer the contents of the pan to a bowl. Add the shredded meat, bulgur, and chopped parsley, and mix. Check and adjust the seasoning.

Stuff and cook the squash
Fill the hollowed out squash with the stuffing, then add the grated Parmesan.

Cook the stuffed squash
Place the squash on the baking sheet with the salt and cook in the oven for at least 30 minutes until the butternut is soft, you can check with the tip of a knife.

Serve
Take the squash out of the oven, arrange on a platter, and serve immediately.

EGG IN POULE AU POT ASPIC

SERVES 4
PREPARATION TIME: 30 MINUTES
COOK TIME: 15 MINUTES

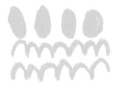

750 milliliters - 3 cups plus 3 1/2
tablespoons chicken broth (see p. 62)
5 sheets (leaves) gelatin
Salt
Freshly ground pepper
2 carrots
4 stalks celery
Olive oil
Leftover chicken from poule au pot
(see p. 62)
White vinegar
4 eggs
1/2 bunch flat-leaf parsley
1/5 bunch chervil
1/2 bunch chives
Fleur de sel

AD - Of course, extra fresh, organic eggs should be used. And well-seasoned broth. This is a good way to use the leftover meat from the chicken carcass after making poule au pot.

PN - This is a complete meal for a family dinner. But also as an appetizer to impress relatives at Sunday lunch.

Make the chicken broth aspic
Remove the layer of fat solidified on the top of the cold broth. Measure out 500 milliliters - 2 cups broth and put into a saucepan. Soak the gelatin in a bowl filled with cold water. When the broth comes to a boil, line a strainer with a damp cloth, place over another saucepan, and strain the broth. Drain the gelatin and add it to the broth. Adjust the seasoning with salt and pepper.

When the broth has cooled somewhat, put one small ladleful of broth into each of four bowls. Refrigerate until set, about 1 hour until the aspic is formed. Set aside the remainder of the aspic.

Prepare the vegetables
In the meantime, peel the onions and carrots, and remove the tough strings from the celery stalks. Finely dice the onions, carrots, and celery. Heat a little olive oil in a sauté pan and sweat them for 10 minutes. Transfer to a dish. Shred the leftover chicken and add to the dish with the vegetables.

Prepare the soft-boiled eggs
Fill a saucepan with a few inches of water to which a splash of vinegar has been added. Bring to a rolling boil. Carefully add the eggs and boil for 5 minutes. Cool and peel the eggs. Place an egg in each bowl with the set broth and arrange the vegetable and meat mixture around it. Lightly heat the remaining aspic and pour it over. Return the bowls to the refrigerator until the aspic hardens.

Finish and serve
Rinse and dry the parsley, chervil, and chives. Pluck the leaves of the parsley and chervil and chop, and cut the chives into short lengths. Place in a small bowl and drizzle the herbs with olive oil and season with fleur de sel.
Top each bowl with some of this salad, make a small cut into the yolk, and serve.

FRIED EGGS AND HEDGEHOG MUSHROOMS

SERVES 4
PREPARATION TIME: 20 MINUTES
COOK TIME: 15 MINUTES

500 grams - 1 pound 2 ounces
hedgehog mushrooms
1/2 bunch flat-leaf parsley
4 cloves garlic
50 grams - 2 ounces Comté
cheese
6 slices sandwich bread
4 thin slices bacon
30 grams - 2 tablespoons
butter
4 eggs
Olive oil
Salt
Freshly ground pepper

AD - This recipe works with other kinds of mushrooms, depending on the season, and also all year with Japanese mushrooms and white mushrooms. If you want to add refinement and if you have a large stove, make this dish using four small frying pans.

PN - Take care when cooking the eggs that the yolk is not overcooked, otherwise it isn't good. One egg per person is enough. I like it when there is cheese in a dish; it adds calcium.

Prepare the mushrooms, parsley, garlic, and Comté cheese
Cut off the mushroom stems, then wash and quickly dry the mushrooms. Rinse, dry, pluck, and chop the parsley leaves. Peel and mince 3 of the garlic cloves. Cut the Comté cheese into small cubes.

Make toast soldiers
Toast the slices of bread. Peel the remaining garlic clove and rub it over the slices of toast, then cut each slice into 4 strips (soldiers).

Cook the mushrooms and eggs
Heat a large frying pan and sweat the slices of bacon, turning them frequently. Add the butter and melt. Add the mushrooms, season lightly with salt, and sweat for 2 minutes. Add the minced garlic and stir.

Cook until the liquid released by the mushrooms has evaporated. Push the contents of the pan evenly to the sides, and break the eggs in the center. Add the cubes of cheese and chopped parsley to the mushrooms. Cook until the egg whites have just set.

Finish and serve
Season with a turn of the pepper mill and serve in the pan together with the garlic-rubbed toast soldiers.

POULE AU POT ("CHICKEN IN A POT")

<u>SERVES 4</u>
<u>PREPARATION TIME: 30 MINUTES</u>
<u>COOK TIME: 1 HOUR</u>
<u>REST TIME: 20 MINUTES</u>

1 whole organic chicken about 1.2 kilograms - 2 pounds 10 ounces
4 carrots
8 turnips
4 leeks
1 head celery
1 onion
1 clove
300 grams - 10 1/2 ounces white mushrooms
Salt
1 sprig thyme
1 bay leaf
4 juniper berries
Freshly ground pepper

AD - This has been a great classic of French cuisine since the time of Henry IV. Carefully save the broth. Put it in the refrigerator and defat it afterward. You can use it for a number of dishes (see pp. 39, 44, 57, 58, 65, 72, 119, 235).

PN - A superb one-dish meal. People often complain that chicken is too fatty, but much of this fat goes into the broth, which you later remove.

Prepare the vegetables
Peel and wash the carrots and turnips but leave whole. Thoroughly wash the leeks. Remove the tough dark green part of the leeks. Wash the head of celery. Divide the head of celery into stalks, remove the tough strings, and cut each stalk in half. Peel the onion and stud with the clove. Quickly rinse and dry the mushrooms, then peel them and cut off their stems.

Cook the chicken and the vegetables
Put the chicken in a large cast-iron pot or Dutch oven. Cover with abundant water and season with salt. Bring to a boil and skim off the foam.

When all the foam is removed, add the carrots, turnips, leeks, celery, studded onion, thyme, bay leaf, and juniper berries. Simmer for 45 minutes. Then add the mushrooms and cook for 15 minutes more. Taste the broth and adjust the seasoning with salt and pepper.

Finish and serve
Let the chicken rest in its cooking liquid for 20 minutes, then transfer it to a cutting board and carve it.

Arrange the pieces of chicken and the vegetables on a hot platter and serve immediately.

63

CHICKEN SALAD WITH SAVORA© MUSTARD

SERVES 4
PREPARATION TIME: 25 MINUTES
COOK TIME: 2 MINUTES

2 red onions
25 grams - 1 ounce/1 1/2
tablespoons honey
100 milliliters - 1/3 cup
plus 1 tablespoon sherry
vinegar
5 red radishes
400 grams - 14 ounces
leftover chicken from poule
au pot (see p. 62)
3 shallots
4 heads Little Gem lettuce
1 bunch chives
1/2 jar Savora® mustard (193
grams - 6 3/4-ounces/3/4 cup)
1 pinch Espelette pepper
5 tablespoons olive oil
Salt

Prepare the pickled onion
Peel and finely slice the onions. Transfer to a heatproof bowl. Combine the honey and vinegar in a small saucepan and place over high level heat. When the mixture is about to come to a boil, pour it over the onions. Stir and set aside.

Prepare the radish slices
Fill a mixing bowl with water and ice cubes. Wash, dry, and peel the radishes. Use a mandoline with safety guard to cut fine slices. As they are cut, plunge them into the ice water to make them crunchy.

Make the chicken salad
Shred the chicken into a bowl. Peel and finely chop the shallots, then add them to the bowl. Separate, rinse, and dry the lettuce leaves. Finely chop the chives. Add the lettuce and chives to the bowl with the chicken and shallots.

In a separate bowl, combine the mustard with a pinch of salt and Espelette pepper. Drizzle in the olive oil while beating with a fork. Pour this dressing over the chicken salad and toss.

Finish
Add the pickled onion to the salad. Toss together, then taste and adjust the seasoning. Serve the salad on plates. Drain the radish slices well and arrange on top. Serve immediately.

AD - I haven't included the traditional croutons in this recipe; I prefer to have a good, crispy baguette to soak up the sauce.

PN - You're right. That way, you eat more bread. You won't need a cheese or dessert after this dish.

FREGOLA, SHRIMP, BASIL, AND ALMONDS

16 tiger shrimp (prawns)
1 bunch basil
1 teaspoon pine nuts
3 tablespoons grated Parmesan cheese
100 milliliters - 1/3 cup plus 1 tablespoon olive oil
20 blanched almonds
1 small onion
Salt
20 grams - 1 1/2 tablespoons butter
250 grams - 9 ounces / 1 1/2 cups medium fregola pasta
Olive oil
Freshly ground pep

AD - Fregola is a variety of pasta from Sardinia. The special thing about it is that it's first shaped into little balls and then toasted in the oven after drying to give it a lovely golden color. It's a real treat.

Clean the shrimp
Peel and devein the shrimp and set aside in a bowl in the refrigerator.

Prepare the pesto and almonds
Rinse and pluck the basil leaves. Place the basil into the jar of a blender with the pine nuts, 1 tablespoon of the grated Parmesan, and the olive oil. Blend until smooth. Transfer to a bowl and set aside. Chop the almonds.

Prepare the pasta
Peel and finely chop the onion. Bring 500 milliliters - 2 cups lightly salted water to a boil.

Heat a little olive oil with 10 grams - 2 teaspoons of the butter in a cast-iron pan and sweat the onion over medium heat without coloring. Add the pasta and stir for 1 minute to coat well with the butter and oil.

Cover with boiling water, mix, and cook until it is absorbed by the pasta, then gradually add the remaining water. The pasta should take about 10 minutes to cook. Season with salt and pepper.

Cook the shrimp
In the meantime, heat a little oil in a frying pan and sauté the shrimp for 1 minute.

Finish and serve
When the pasta is cooked, remove from the heat. Add the remaining 10 grams - 2 teaspoons butter, the remaining 2 tablespoons Parmesan, the pesto, and chopped almonds.

Return the pan to the heat for a few seconds while stirring. Add the shrimp and mix gently. Serve immediately and very hot from the pan.

KONJAC FRITTATA

SERVES 4
PREPARATION TIME: 10 MINUTES
COOK TIME: 10 MINUTES

250 grams -9 ounces shirataki
(konjac) noodles
Salt
1 red onion
1 clove garlic
150 grams - 5 1/2 ounces
white mushrooms
2 handfuls red orache leaves
2 handfuls baby spinach
2 eggs
100 milliliters - 1/3 cup
plus 1 tablespoon lowfat (2%)
milk
Olive oil
Freshly ground pepper

AD - Konjac is a type of yam that has been grown in Asia for thousands of years. It is very large, growing up to 80 centimeters (over 2 1/2 feet) in circumference. It's ground into a very fine flour, which is used to make shirataki noodles. They can be found at Asian grocery stores and online.

PN - Konjac consists of a fiber that has great powers of absorption. It contains no carbohydrates, practically no calories, and it fills the stomach. Every assiduous dieter knows about it. They're in for a treat with this dish, chef.

Prepare the noodles
Put the noodles in a strainer and rinse under running water. Bring lightly salted water to a boil in a sauce-pan and immerse the noodles in the boiling water for 1 minute. Drain immediately. Spread out over a dish cloth or paper towels to dry.

Prepare the vegetables
Peel and thinly slice the onion and garlic. Cut off the earthy stems and quickly wash and dry the mushrooms. Remove the stems, and wash and dry the orache and spinach.

Make the frittata
Break the eggs into a bowl, add the milk, and beat well. Heat a little olive oil in a frying pan and cook the onion, garlic, and mushrooms until browned, about 3 minutes. Season with salt and stir. Add the noodles and mix well with the vegetables.

Add the egg and milk mixture. Tilt the pan to distribute the mixture very evenly. Spread half of the salad greens over the mixture. Cook gently until the egg is congealed.

Finish and serve
Put the remaining salad greens in a small bowl, season with salt and a turn of the pepper mill, and 1 teaspoon of olive oil. Toss to coat. Remove the frittata from the heat and spread the salad over the frittata. Serve imme-diately in the pan.

PEARL BARLEY AND BLACK TRUMPET MUSHROOMS

SERVES 4
PREPARATION TIME: 15 MINUTES
COOK TIME: 35 MINUTES

200 grams - 7 ounces black trumpet mushrooms
300 grams - 10 1/2 ounces/ 1 1/2 cups pearl barley
Salt
1 onion
1 clove garlic
Olive oil
Freshly ground pepper
1/2 bunch flat-leaf parsley
10 grams - 2 teaspoons butter
1 (150-gram - 5.3-ounce) container plain Greek yogurt
1 pinch Espelette pepper

AD - Pearl barley are barley grains that have been mechanically polished to give them an even and uniform shape.

PN - This means that its hull has been removed, and with it most of its fiber, vitamins, and minerals. What remains is basically carbohydrate. Other vegetables, either in a soup or as an appetizer, are needed to compensate. Mushrooms aren't enough.

Prepare the mushrooms
Trim the mushroom stems. Immerse the mushrooms in warm water and move them around. Repeat the operation until the water turns completely clear. Dry the mushrooms in a salad spinner.

Cook the pearl barley
Put the pearl barley in a strainer and rinse under running water. Put 1 L - 4 1/2 cups salted water in a saucepan, and bring to a boil. Add the barley, cover with a lid, and simmer for 30 minutes.

Cook the black trumpet mushrooms
Peel and mince the onion and garlic clove. Heat a little olive oil in a frying pan. Cook the onion and garlic until browned, about 2 minutes. Next, add the mushrooms. Sauté for 5 minutes. Season with a little salt and with pepper.

Finish and serve
Wash, dry, pluck, and chop the parsley leaves. Drain the barley and return it to the saucepan. Add the mushroom mixture to the barley and mix gently. Add the butter and stir gently until melted, and then add the yogurt. Stir. Season with Espelette pepper and add the chopped parsley. Check and adjust the seasoning with salt. If the mixture is too dry, add a little water. Serve immediately from a large bowl or in individual dishes.

CRISPY POLENTA WITH PARMESAN AND SAGE

SERVES 4
PREPARATION TIME: 10 MINUTES
COOK TIME: 50 MINUTES
CHILL TIME: 3 HOURS

1 liter - 4 1/4 cups poule au pot (chicken) broth (see p. 62)
200 grams - 7 ounces/1 1/2 cups polenta
2 cloves garlic
1 bunch sage
100 milliliters - 1/3 cup plus 1 tablespoon olive oil, plus extra for pan
200 grams - 7 ounces/2 1/3 cups grated Parmesan cheese
Salt
Freshly ground pepper

AD - Buy non-GMO polenta from an organic food store. And, more particularly, don't be lured into buying instant polenta that cooks in 5 minutes; it's pretty awful!

PN - Parmesan is one of the cheeses with the highest calcium content. Fifty grams (about 1/2 cup) per person is enough to cover your daily allowance.

Prepare the polenta

Put the chicken broth into a cast-iron pot or Dutch oven and bring to a boil. Sprinkle in the polenta white stirring with a whisk. Boil for 5 minutes while stirring constantly.

Use a flexible spatula (scraper) to clean the sides of the pan well and to push all of the polenta to the center. Cover the pan with a lid, turn the heat down to low, and cook for 40 minutes more, stirring frequently.

Finish the polenta

Peel the garlic and remove the green core; mince the garlic. Rinse, dry, pluck, and mince the sage leaves. When the polenta is cooked, gradually add the olive oil while stirring with a spatula. Add the Parmesan, garlic, and sage. Combine thoroughly. Season with salt and pepper.

Line a large frying pan with plastic wrap (cling film) and cover with the firm polenta to a thickness of about 3 centimeters - 1 1/4 inches. Cover with another sheet of plastic wrap and tap the pan a few times to distribute the polenta evenly in the pan. Refrigerate for at least 3 hours.

Serve

Turn the polenta out onto a tray and remove the plastic wrap. Heat a little olive oil in the frying pan and return the polenta to the pan. Brown for 2 minutes, then slide the polenta out onto a large plate; cover with another large plate, flip the plates, and slide the polenta back into the pan to brown the other side. Serve from the frying pan.

RICE

On average, 14 metric tons (about 15 1/2 tons) of rice are eaten in the world every second. After wheat, this is the most widely grown grain, particularly in hot and humid regions of the world, because rice grows with the base of its stalk in water and its top requires plenty of sunlight. Where does it come from? Nobody knows exactly, but what is certain is that it has been grown in Asia for more than 10,000 years; its cultivation in paddy fields was developed in China; it arrived in Greece in 340 BC; and it later spread around the Mediterranean region. Rice is traditionally sown in nurseries and then transplanted. The fields are flooded when the rice plants are 20-30 centimeters (8-12 inches) tall, then drained when their clusters of flowers wilt. The 30-100 grains from each plant are then harvested. This traditional cultivation has been industrialized: Seeds are sown by plane, and there are varieties that don't need transplanting, mechanical harvesting, and so on. And this takes place between one and four times a year, depending on the two thousand varieties that are now grown.

➥ VARIETIES AND SEASONS

Long-grain varieties of rice have grains of varying lengths that remain firm after cooking. They include, among others, basmati, fragrant rice varieties, red rice, Black Venere, and all the sticky or glutinous varieties.

Round-grain varieties of rice absorb more water during cooking and so take on a creamy appearance. Among them are risotto rices (Arborio, Carnaroli, Belo, and Vialone Nano), the Japanese Koshihikari variety, and Spanish Bomba rice. These different varieties are available throughout the year.

➥ CHOOSING AND STORAGE

Freshly harvested from the paddy to parboiled in a bag, there are many processes that rice undergoes, in which its outer layers are gradually removed. It can be stored for up to one year in a dry place, although brown rice only keeps for six months.

➥ NUTRITION

Rice is mainly a source of complex carbohydrates that contains some protein, although no gluten or fats. The more it is refined, the lower its vitamin and mineral content.

➥ USES AND COMBINATIONS

There are countless savory and sweet dishes that contain rice, which can be combined with everything. It is also used to make derivative products: flour, pasta, precooked flakes, puffed rice, spring roll wrappers, beverages (rice milk, sake, mirin, Shaoxing wine), vinegar, and syrup.

RICE, CORN, AND CHILI PILAF

SERVES 4
PREPARATION TIME: 10 MINUTES
COOK TIME: 20 MINUTES
REST TIME: 10 MINUTES

3 new onions or 1 white onion
2 sweet chili peppers
450 milliliters - 2 cups poule au pot (chicken) broth (see p. 62)
4 tablespoons olive oil
300 grams - 10 1/2 ounces/1 1/2 cups round-grain rice
Salt
100 grams - 3 1/2 ounces/2/3 cup cooked corn kernels
1 teaspoon hot curry powder
1 handful baby spinach
Freshly ground pepper

AD - If you don't have any chicken broth or stock, just use water.

PN - Chili is very good for your health and for a balanced diet. It contains plenty of protective antioxidants, such as capsaicin, which produces a feeling of being full. With all the carbs provided by the rice and corn, you won't feel hunger pangs during the afternoon.

Cook the rice
Preheat the oven to 180°C - 350°F (gas mark 4). Peel and mince the new onions. Finely slice the chili peppers. Put the chicken broth in a saucepan and place over high heat.

Heat the olive oil in a cast-iron pan over medium heat and sweat the onions for about 2 minutes while stirring. Add the rice with a pinch of salt and cook for 2 minutes over low heat, stirring well until translucent. Add the corn kernels, curry powder, and sliced chili peppers, then add the warm chicken broth.

Bring to a boil, cover the pan with a lid, and place in the oven for 17 minutes. Let the rice rest for 10 minutes. Season with salt and pepper.

Prepare the spinach
While the rice is resting, remove the spinach stems, then wash and dry the spinach leaves.

Finish and serve
Arrange the spinach leaves over the rice after it has rested. Do not mix. Serve from the pan.

SOBA NOODLES WITH FRUIT AND VEGETABLES

SERVES 4
PREPARATION TIME: 20 MINUTES
COOK TIME: 15 MINUTES

Juice of 1 lemon
2 Curé pears (or another variety but the pear must be large and not too mature)
2 avocados
1 red onion
1 yellow squash
1 yellow beet (beetroot)
1 bunch chives
1/4 bunch flat-leaf parsley
5-centimeter- - 2-inch-length ginger
Olive oil
Salt
300 grams - 10 1/2 ounces soba noodles
2 tablespoons Barolo vinegar
1 pinch Espelette pepper

AD - Soba are artisan Japanese noodles made using buckwheat flour (soba being the japanese word for this grain). They can be found at Japanese grocery stores and online.

PN - Buckwheat is gluten-free. It has plenty of dietary fiber, phenolic antioxidants, and minerals too, including a lot of magnesium and copper. This grain should be eaten more often.

Prepare the fruits
Juice the lemon over a bowl of water. Peel, halve, and core the pears. Place the pear halves in the lemon water. Cut open the avocados. Remove the seed and scoop out the flesh with a spoon. Cut into large chunks.

Prepare the vegetables
Peel and finely slice the onion. Peel the piece of squash, cut it into chunks, and set aside. Peel the beet and use a mandoline with safety guard to cut it into thick slices. Rinse, dry, and mince the chives. Rinse, dry, and pluck the parsley leaves. Peel and grate the ginger.

Heat a little olive oil in a sauté pan, and fry the avocados, onion, squash, and beet. Remove the vegetables from the pan when softened (check with the tip of a knife) and transfer to a dish.

Cook the noodles
Bring 1 L - 4 1/2 cups salted water to a boil in a saucepan. Sprinkle in the noodles, stir, and cook for 2-3 minutes after the water comes back to a boil. Strain and transfer to a dish. Drizzle with a little olive oil and mix well.

Finish and serve
Return the cooked vegetables to the sauté pan. Deglaze the pan with vinegar, then add the noodles, ginger, Espelette pepper, chives, and parsley. Gently mix together. Serve on plates or from a serving dish.

BUCKWHEAT, LEEK, HAM, AND MOZZARELLA CLAFOUTIS

SERVES 4
PREPARATION TIME: 15 MINUTES
COOK TIME: 35 MINUTES

4 medium leeks
1 ball Mozzarella di Bufala Campana cheese
1 thick slice ham
3 eggs
20 grams - 2 3/4 tablespoons flour
25 grams - 3 1/2 tablespoons buckwheat flour
150 grams - 5 1/2 ounces/1 1/2 cups plus 1 tablespoon almond meal (ground almonds)
200 milliliters - 3/4 cup plus 1 tablespoon *lait ribot* or buttermilk
250 grams - 1 cup crème fraîche
2 grams - 1/3 teaspoon salt
Butter for greasing

Prepare the leeks
Cut off the roots and the dark green parts of the leeks. Fill a large bowl with cold water. Cut through the leeks along their entire length, leaving the root end intact. Make another lengthwise cut to quarter each leek. Plunge in the cold water. Shake well and drain. Cut into slices about 5 millimeters - 1/4 inch thick.
Bring water to a boil in a couscoussier. Put the leek slices in the steamer basket, steam for about 5 minutes, and then transfer to a container.

Make the clafoutis
Preheat the oven to 180°C - 350°F (gas mark 4). Cut the mozzarella ball into a 1-centimeter - 1/2-inch dice. Cut the ham into thick strips.

In a bowl, mix the eggs, both types of flour, almond meal, *lait ribot*, crème fraîche, and salt. Add the leek and ham pieces. Mix well.

Grease a tart mold with butter. Fill with the contents of the bowl and scatter the diced mozzarella over the top. Bake for 20–30 minutes.

Serve
Serve the clafoutis in the mold as soon as it comes out of the oven.

AD - Buy real mozzarella, Mozzarella di Bufala Campana, which is made from buffalo milk. Cow's milk mozzarella is made with a more or less industrial process; it's tasteless and very rubbery.

PN - Eggs, ham, and cheese, a good combination of animal protein, plus carbohydrate and fat—this is a very good and complete dish. A salad to accompany and a piece of fruit afterward is sufficient.

TORTA PASQUALINA (EASTER PIE) WITH MUSHROOMS

7 medium porcini mushrooms
4 large white mushrooms
100 grams - 3 1/2 ounces black trumpet mushrooms
Olive oil
200 grams - 7 ounces baby spinach
1 clove garlic
1/2 bunch flat-leaf parsley
1/2 bunch chervil
1/2 bunch chives
2 eggs, plus 1 yolk, divided
50 grams - 2 ounces/1/2 cup grated Parmesan cheese
3 pinches juniper berry powder
1 Basic pastry (see p. 367)
Salt
Freshly ground pepper

Prepare the mushrooms
Cut off the base of the stems from the porcini and white mushrooms. Clean the black trumpet mushrooms. Very quickly wash the mushrooms and dry them. Cut them into pieces about 3 centimeters - 1 1/4 inches thick.
Heat a little olive oil in a sauté pan and sweat the mushrooms for 5 minutes. Transfer to a mixing bowl.

Prepare the spinach and herbs
Wash the baby spinach. Peel the garlic clove. Prick the clove with a fork and leave it on the end. Heat a little olive oil in a frying pan and wilt the spinach, stirring with the garlic clove. Transfer to a dish.
When cool, coarsely chop. Add the spinach to the mushrooms. Rinse, pluck, and mince the parsley and chervil leaves; mince the chives. Add the herbs to the bowl.

Make the filling
Combine the eggs with the Parmesan and mix. Season with juniper berry powder, salt, and pepper.

Make the pie
Preheat the oven to 220 C - 425°F (gas mark 7). Dilute the egg yolk with a little water. Roll out the pastry into two disks measuring 25 centimeters (10 inches) and 30 centimeters (12 inches) in diameter, respectively. Transfer the smaller disk to a baking sheet lined with parchment paper and mound filling over it.

Brush the edges with the egg yolk, cover with the other disk, and press the edges down with your fingers to seal. Brush the pie with egg yolk and make a hole in the center. Place in the oven, lower the temperature to 180°C - 350°F (gas mark 4). Bake for 15–20 minutes.

Finish and serve
When you take the pie out of the oven, slide it on a dish and let it rest for 30 minutes in a warm place. Serve warm.

BRAISED CARROTS WITH LEMON, CILANTRO, AND CHILI

SERVES 4
PREPARATION TIME: 10 MINUTES
COOK TIME: 35 MINUTES

12-16 small new carrots, with greens (tops)
1 sweet chili pepper
1 teaspoon coriander seeds
4 tablespoons olive oil
Salt
1 clove garlic
2 sprigs cilantro (coriander)
1 organic, unwaxed lemon

Prepare the carrots
Preheat the oven to 170°C - 340°F (gas mark 3-4). Wash the carrots. Keep 5 centimeters - 2 inches of their greens. Put into an ovenproof dish. Finely slice the chili and add to the dish. Put the coriander seeds in a pepper mill and grind over the carrots with one turn of the pepper mill. Drizzle with the olive oil and season with salt. Toss. Distribute the carrots evenly in the dish.

Cook the carrots
Place the carrots in the oven and cook until they soften (you can check with the tip of a knife), about 30 minutes. Peel, chop, and add the garlic to the dish. Return to the oven for 5 minutes.

Prepare the cilantro
In the meantime, rinse, dry, and pluck the cilantro leaves. Put the leaves in a bowl and use scissors to coarsely cut them up.

Finish
Remove the dish from the oven and grate lemon zest over the carrots. Squeeze the juice and drizzle it over the carrots. Then scatter the cilantro evenly over the top. Serve from the hot dish.

AD - Adjust the number of carrots depending on their size, and on everyone's appetite, naturally.

PN - Eating carrots is supposed to make you kind and give you rosy cheeks. They're full of carotenes, those wonderful antioxidant molecules that protect so much and tint your skin a little.

ROASTED TANDOORI CAULIFLOWER WITH LEMON

SERVES 4
PREPARATION TIME: 10 MINUTES
COOK TIME: 48 MINUTES

1 large cauliflower
Salt
3 organic, unwaxed lemons
15 grams - 2 tablespoons
tandoori spice blend
2 grams - 1/3 teaspoon coarse
salt
100 milliliters - 1/3 cup
plus 1 tablespoon olive oil

Prepare the cauliflower

Remove the outer leaves from the cauliflower, but keep the more tender leaves around it. Wash the cauliflower. Bring a large pot of salted water to a boil. Immerse the cauliflower in the boiling water for 8 minutes, drain well, and transfer to an ovenproof dish.

Make the spice oil

Grate the zest from the lemons into a bowl. Add the tandoori spice blend, coarse salt, and olive oil, and mix.

Cook the cauliflower

Set the oven to 200°C - 400°F (gas mark 6). Brush the cauliflower on all sides with the spice oil. Pour the rest of the oil over it. Roast until tender, about 40 minutes (a knife should easily pierce the cauliflower).

Serve

Remove the dish from the oven and serve in the hot dish.

AD - If you see that the cauliflower is turning brown very quickly, cover it with aluminum foil.

PN - Don't waste the zested lemons. Immediately squeeze them and make a nice lemonade, full of vitamin C, as a drink before your meal.

BRAISED ENDIVES WITH BLACKBERRIES

SERVES 4
PREPARATION TIME: 10 MINUTES
COOK TIME: 40 MINUTES

9 heads endive (chicory)
1 white onion
1 clove pink garlic
Olive oil
Salt
300 grams - 10 1/2 ounces
(about 2 trays/punnets)
blackberries
250 milliliters - 1 cup
Riesling wine
Freshly ground pepper
10 grams - 2 teaspoons butter
3 pinches Espelette pepper

AD - Take advantage of the first endives and the last blackberries of the season to make this dish. The sweetness of the Riesling tones down the bitterness of the endives and the slight sourness of the blackberries. And in winter, why not replace the blackberries with clementines?

PN - Blackberries are full of all kinds of antioxidants, and endives have quite a few themselves. They have few calories. With so little fat, this is a particularly light dish. I love mixing cooked and raw in the same dish.

Prepare the endives and blackberries
Wash and dry the endive heads. Set one aside. Peel and slice the onion into thin rounds. Leave the garlic clove unpeeled, but crush lightly.

Heat a little olive oil in a cast-iron pan on medium heat. Put the 8 remaining endive heads, the onion rounds, and the garlic clove in the pan. Season lightly with salt and cook for 20 minutes, browning the endives on all sides.

In the meantime, select the best blackberries and hull if necessary. When the endives are golden, deglaze the pan with the wine. Mix well with a flexible spatula (scraper). Season with salt and pepper. Cover the pan with a lid and simmer for 5 minutes more. Then add two thirds of the berries. Mix gently, without crushing them. Replace the lid and cook for 10 minutes more. Finally, add the butter and stir gently to thicken the cooking liquid.

Prepare the endive slices
While the endives are cooking, wash and dry the reserved head. Use a mandoline with safety guard to cut it into fine slices. Transfer to a bowl, add the remaining berries, drizzle with olive oil, and add the Espelette pepper. Gently mix together.

Serve
Serve the endives in the pan, and the endive and blackberry salad separately.

ROASTED BUTTERNUT SQUASH

SERVES 4
PREPARATION TIME: 30 MINUTES
COOK TIME: 1 HOUR 30 MINUTES

1 butternut squash
1/4 bunch mint
1/4 bunch flat-leaf parsley
1 slice bacon, about 1
centimter - 1/2 inch thick
5 anchovy fillets in oil
2 tablespoons pitted black
olives
1 clove garlic
500 grams - 2 1/4 cups
coarse salt
Salt
Pepper
Olive oil

AD - A waiter's friend corkscrew is
an object resembling a corkscrew and
bottle opener; you're sure to have one
in your kitchen.

PN - What an imagination you have,
chef! Your roasted squash is so much
fun. Well, you need a bit of patience
to fill in all the holes, but it's worth
the effort to impress your friends.

Prepare the squash
Wash and dry the squash. Cut off the top third. Use a teaspoon to remove all the seeds.

Wash, dry, and pluck the mint and parsley leaves. Set aside two thirds in a bowl for finishing. Cut the bacon into about 3-cm- - 1 1/4-inch-long lardons.

Halve the anchovy fillets and quarter the olives lengthwise. Peel the garlic clove and cut it lengthwise into 6-9 pieces.

Use a waiter's friend corkscrew (or a plain corkscrew) to dig about 20 holes into the flesh of the squash, taking care not to pierce the skin. Fill the holes with the remaining third of herbs, and the lardons, anchovies, olives, and garlic. Press the filling in gently with your finger.

Cook the squash
Preheat the oven to 180°C - 350°F (gas mark 4). Cover the bottom of an ovenproof dish with coarse salt. Season the squash with salt and pepper, and drizzle with olive oil. Cover with the top of the squash.

Roast in the oven for 1 hour–1 hour 30 minutes, depending on the size of the squash. Check that the squash is cooked by piercing it with a knife. It should slide in easily.

Finish and serve
Drizzle the bowl of reserved herbs with olive oil and a pinch of salt, and mix.

Remove the squash from the oven and rest for about 10 minutes. Lift off the lid, add the herb–olive oil mixture, then replace the lid. Serve the squash in the dish. Allow guests to serve themselves.

CELERY AND ORANGE SALAD

SERVES 4
PREPARATION TIME: 15 MINUTES

1 head celery with 10-12 stalks
1 red onion
4 blood oranges
100 grams - 3 1/2 ounces feta cheese
4 sprigs flat-leaf parsley
4 tablespoons olive oil
1 tablespoon wine vinegar
Salt
Freshly ground pepper
2 tablespoons pitted Nice black olives

Prepare the celery and onion
Wash the celery stalks. Pluck off the small yellow leaves and set aside. Remove the strings from the stalks and use a mandoline with safety guard to slice them into strips. Transfer to a salad bowl. Peel and slice the onion into very fine rounds. Add the onion to the bowl.

Prepare the oranges and cheese
Supreme the oranges over a bowl to catch the juice. Put each segment in the salad bowl as it is cut from the oranges.

Squeeze the juice from the orange scraps. Cut the cheese into small cubes and add them to the salad bowl.

Finish the salad
Rinse, dry, pluck, and mince the parsley leaves. Add the olive oil and vinegar to the bowl with the orange juice. Season with salt and pepper. Gently mix the contents of the salad bowl. Add the olives and parsley. Pour the dressing over the salad and toss.

Serve from the salad bowl or divide among 4 plates.

AD - If this salad is served very cool, it will be even tastier. If you are using organic, unwaxed oranges, you can grate a little zest over the salad at the last minute.

PN - I already said somewhere that celery was reputed to be an aphrodisiac. This salad can be appreciated on a fall weekend before a short siesta.

APPLES

Apples have existed for thousands of years and are found throughout the world. The French name *pomme* comes from the Latin word *poma*, which means fruit. If there is a universal symbol charged with all kinds of meanings—sin, discord, femininity, love, wisdom, innovation—it's the apple. This round fruit with relatively crisp, sweet, and sour flesh encases five rigid cavities in its center, each housing two seeds. Its skin can be green, yellow, or red, depending on the variety.

VARIETIES AND SEASONS

More than two thousand varieties of apple trees have been counted, although only thirty or so are grown and produce apples year-round. The harvested fruits are placed in cold storage for several months in order to stagger the time when they come to market. Most apples are picked in September and October. Fuji, Gala, Golden Delicious, Granny Smith, among others, are most commonly found at farmers' markets.

CHOOSING AND STORAGE

A good-quality apple has smooth skin, without blemishes, and a very green stalk. It can be kept in the open air for several days; it can be kept in the refrigerator if it is too ripe or if the weather is too warm.

NUTRITION

The combination of dietary fiber, different minerals, and a large number of polyphenols contained by apples make them an all-around health food, with a benefits to intestinal health, cholesterol, blood sugar, and the respiratory tract. There are countless scientific studies that have proved the old saying "an apple a day keeps the doctor away." This would be true if apples weren't, unfortunately, filled with pesticides, and subjected to so many treatments. It is in your best interest to eat organic apples.

USES AND COMBINATIONS

Whether sweet or savory, hot or cold, apples can be cooked and prepared in thousands of ways. They go with practically everything.

TURNIP, APPLE, GARAM MASALA, AND PUMPKINSEED SALAD

SERVES 4
PREPARATION TIME: 15 MINUTES
COOK TIME: 5 MINUTES

2 bunches baby turnips
3 apples
1 organic, unwaxed lemon
1 organic, unwaxed lime
75 grams - 2 2/3 ounces/1/2
cup pumpkinseeds
Olive oil
1 teaspoon garam masala
spice mix
Salt
Freshly ground pepper

Prepare the turnips and apples
Wash, peel, and halve the turnips. Peel, quarter, and core the apples. Squeeze the lemon and lime juices into a salad bowl.

Use a mandoline with safety guard to cut the turnips into thin rounds and the apple quarters into batons. As they are cut, transfer to the salad bowl and mix with the juice to prevent them from turning brown.

Prepare the pumpkinseeds
Brush a frying pan lightly with olive oil and place over high heat. Toast the pumpkinseeds until they are light golden and crispy. Transfer to paper towels.

Finish the salad
Add the garam masala spice mix to the salad bowl. Drizzle generously with olive oil and toss. Season with salt and pepper. Add the toasted pumpkinseeds and serve immediately from the salad bowl or divide among 4 plates.

AD - Add the pumpkinseeds at the last minute. Otherwise, they'll absorb moisture and lose their crispiness.

PN - Turnips and apples contain very little vitamin C. Luckily, this is provided by the citrus, which is good because it balances the dish.

FALL VEGETABLE TARTARE

SERVES 4
PREPARATION TIME: 20 MINUTES

1 small white cabbage
3 small new carrots with green tops
4 large porcini mushrooms
8 fresh figs
8 walnut halves
2 egg yolks
1 (150-gram - 5.3-ounce) container plain yogurt
2 teaspoons Dijon mustard
6 tablespoons olive oil
Salt
Freshly ground pepper

Prepare the cabbage and carrots
Separate, wash, and dry the cabbage leaves. Remove the central rib, roll up the leaves, and cut them into thin strips. Wash and peel the carrots, cut off the ends, and grate them. Combine the cabbage and carrots in a deep earthenware bowl.

Prepare the mushrooms and figs
Peel the stems of the mushrooms. Quickly rinse the mushrooms under running water and dry with paper towels. Separate the stems from the caps and set aside the caps in the refrigerator. Cut the stems into a small dice and add to the bowl with the cabbage and carrots. Cut each fig into five slices and transfer to a plate.

Chop the walnuts
Put the walnut halves on a cutting board and coarsely chop them. Add them to the bowl.

Make the sauce
Combine the egg yolks, yogurt, and mustard in a bowl. Whisk thoroughly, then gradually whisk in the olive oil. Season with salt and pepper.

Finish the tartare
Add the fig slices to the bowl and drizzle with the sauce. Gently mix so as not to crush the figs.

Place a ring mold with a diameter of 10 centimeters - 4 inches on each plate and fill with the tartare. Remove the mold and slice the mushroom caps directly over the tartare using a mandoline with safety guard.

AD - You should choose young mushrooms. You can tell them apart by the color of the sponge under their caps, which should be very white. If you can't find any porcinis, replace them with two handfuls of shiitake mushrooms.

PN - As the sauce is made using egg yolks and yogurt, you already have a source of animal protein. Take this into account when planning your meal. Pasta wouldn't be a bad choice after this vegetable tartare.

ROTISSERIE PINEAPPLE

SERVES 4
PREPARATION TIME: 20 MINUTES
COOK TIME: 40 MINUTES

1 Victoria pineapple or ripe
organic variety
2 tablespoons creamed honey
1 pinch ground star anise

Prepare the pineapple
Preheat the oven to 220 C - 425°F (gas mark 7). Use a large serrated knife to cut off the bottom of the pineapple to create a stable base. Stand the pineapple, then pass the knife blade under the skin, well behind the thorns, and turn the fruit regularly as you peel. Next, use a paring knife to remove the eyes, which are set in a series of diagonal lines. Carve out the eyes in grooves that follow these lines around the pineapple.

Insert a rotisserie spit firmly through the center of the pineapple, then spread honey over all sides and sprinkle with ground star anise.

Roast the pineapple
Set the spit inside the oven and place a tray under the pineapple to collect the juices it releases when cooking. Start the rotisserie and roast for about 40 minutes.

Use a brush to regularly baste the pineapple with its juices.

Serve
Remove the spit. Serve the pineapple on a tray. Carve slices in front of your guests.

AD - I love rotisserie cooking. It's so easy, natural, and healthy. You need a very ripe pineapple. Pull on one of its leaves; if it comes out easily, then the fruit is ripe.

PN - If your oven doesn't have a rotisserie feature, roast the pineapple on a tray and turn it over several times so that you can baste it well.

KIWI-MINT SMOOTHIE

MAKES 1
PREPARATION TIME: 10 MINUTES

3 kiwis
1 sprig mint
33 milliliters - 2 1/4
tablespoons *lait ribot* or
buttermilk
1 teaspoon honey
3 ice cubes
1/2 organic, unwaxed lime

Peel the kiwis and cut them into chunks. Put them in the jar of a blender.

Rinse, dry, and pluck the mint leaves. Add the leaves to the jar, followed by the *lait ribot* and honey. Finally, add the ice cubes. Blend until smooth.

Immediately pour the smoothie into a large glass. Grate lime zest over it. Mix well and serve.

AD - This is the basic recipe for a whole range of smoothies. You'll have fun making up new ones with different fruits year-round. Drink immediately, otherwise they lose their freshness and flavor.

PN - Lait ribot makes a change from ordinary smoothies. Good idea, chef! I like them a lot because they're a good source of calcium. This one gives you a shot of vitamin C thanks to the kiwi and mint. If you drink this smoothie in the morning, you'll be in top form all day long.

HAZELNUT CAKE WITH LUPIN FLOUR

MAKES 1 CAKE
PREPARATION TIME: 20 MINUTES
COOK TIME: 40 MINUTES

30 grams - 1/4 cup hazelnuts
40 grams - 1/3 cup whole wheat flour
150 grams - 5 1/2 ounces/ 1 1/4 cups lupin (or any gluten-free) flour
10 grams - 2 1/2 teaspoons baking powder
50 grams - 3 1/2 tablespoons hazelnut praline
30 grams - 2 1/2 tablespoons superfine (caster) sugar
1/2 teaspoon ground cinnamon
1/2 teaspoon ground ginger
4 tablespoons olive oil
5 eggs
250 milliliters - 1 cup lowfat (2%) milk
Butter and flour for pan

AD - Lupin is a legume (pulse), like peas and soybeans, that has long been used as cattle feed. It produces superb flowers, followed by beans. Some time ago it was determined that they could be turned into flour.

PN - This cake is ideal for a child's afternoon snack, and also to accompany a fruit salad or to round off a meal that doesn't contain a lot of starchy, carbohydrate-heavy food.

Roast the hazelnuts

Preheat the oven to 150°C - 300°F (gas mark 2). Put the walnuts on a clean cloth on a cutting board or your work surface. Fold the cloth over and hit the hazelnuts with a rolling pin, then roll it over the nuts to crush them. Transfer the crushed nuts to a baking sheet. Roast them in the oven, shaking the pan occasionally, until they are golden, about 10 minutes. Set aside.

Make the cake batter

Raise the oven temperature to 180°C - 350°F (gas mark 4). Combine the flours, baking powder, praline, and sugar in a mixing bowl. Mix well with a flexible spatula (scraper). Add the cinnamon and ginger, then mix again.

Make a well in the dry ingredients, pour in the olive oil and mix. Then add the eggs one at a time, mixing after each addition. Add the milk and mix the batter until it becomes very smooth.

Bake the cake

Grease a loaf pan that is 30 centimeters – 12 inches long with butter, then dust it with flour. Pour in the batter. Tap the pan several times to spread the batter out evenly and to remove any air bubbles. Cover evenly with the toasted hazelnuts.

Bake for 30 minutes. Check that the cake is cooked by pricking the center with a toothpick or knife. It should come out clean.

Finish

Let the cake cool, then unmold onto a platter.

CRUNCHY CEREAL COOKIES

SERVES 4-6
PREPARATION TIME: 10 MINUTES
COOK TIME: 15 MINUTES
CHILL TIME: 12 HOURS

250 grams - 8 3/4 ounces/2 3/4 cups oatmeal
500 grams - 1 pound 2 ounces/6 cups muesli
3 tablespoons rice flour
200 grams - 7 ounces/3/4 cup plus 1 tablespoon acacia honey
6 grams - 2 1/3 teaspoons Espelette pepper
4 grams - 1 1/2 teaspoons ground cinnamon

Prepare the cereals a day ahead
Combine the oatmeal, muesli, and rice flower in a bowl. Add 600 milliliters - 2 1/2 cups hot water and mix. Refrigerate, covered with plastic wrap, for 12 hours.

Make the cookies
Preheat the oven to 160°C - 325°F (gas mark 3). Add the honey, Espelette pepper, and cinnamon to the bowl with the cereals. Mix, then spread the mixture out over a nonstick baking sheet.

Bake until the cookie is quite dry, 10–15 minutes.

Finish
Break the cookie into pieces. Store in a dry place until it is time to enjoy them.

AD - There's nothing easier than making these cookies. Much better and cheaper than store-bought. They go particularly well with stewed mandarins and mango (see p. 189) and the red pepper sorbet (see p. 348).

PN - These have dietary fiber, minerals, and heaps of energy-giving carbohydrates. An excellent afternoon snack for children and accompaniment to a simple fruit salad.

TAPIOCA FLOUR CREPES

SERVES 6-8
PREPARATION TIME: 10 MINUTES
COOK TIME: 15 MINUTES

200 grams - 7 ounces/1 3/4 sticks butter
300 grams - 10 1/2 ounces/2 1/4 cups tapioca flour
50 grams - 1 3/4 ounces/1/3 cup plus 1 tablespoon whole wheat flour
12 grams - 2 teaspoons salt
1 liter - 4 1/4 cups lowfat (2%) milk
Peanut oil
1 hunk bread

Make the crêpe batter
Cut the butter into pieces and melt in a saucepan over medium heat until it has a brown color (a *beurre noisette* - brown butter with a light hazelnut flavor).

Combine the flours in a deep bowl. Add the salt and mix well. Gradually add the milk while whisking constantly. Then whisk in the melted butter.

Cook the crêpes
Grease a nonstick crêpe pan using a hunk of bread soaked in peanut oil. Pour in a small ladle of batter.

Cook the crêpe for 2 minutes, flip it over, and cook the other side for 1 minute. Transfer to a dish and keep warm. Cook the other crêpes the same way.

AD - Why tapioca flour? Because it makes the crêpes incomparably crisp on the outside and a soft on the inside. Once you've tried out this recipe, you'll stick with it.

PN - Fill the crêpes with hazelnut spread (see p. 113) or stewed mandarins and mango (see p. 189) and serve with a fruit salad.

RICE PUDDING WITH COCONUT MILK AND PINEAPPLE

SERVES 4
PREPARATION TIME: 15 MINUTES
COOK TIME: 20 MINUTES

700 milliliters - 3 cups
lowfat (2%) milk
150 grams - 5 1/4 ounces/3/4
cup round-grain rice
40 grams - 3 tablespoons
honey
400 milliliters - 1 2/3 cups
coconut milk
1 Victoria pineapple
1 organic, unwaxed lime

Make the rice pudding
Bring the milk to a boil in a saucepan, remove from the heat, sprinkle in the rice, and stir. Add the honey, stir again, and return the saucepan to the heat. Simmer for 20 minutes.

Turn off the heat and add the coconut milk. Mix well and let it rest in the saucepan.

Prepare the pineapple
While the rice is cooking, peel the pineapple (see p. 101), remove all the eyes, and cut into slices. Remove the hard core and cut the slices into a small dice. Transfer to a mixing bowl. Grate lime zest over the pineapple. Toss well.

Finish and serve
Add the pineapple to the warm rice pudding and mix gently. Serve in bowls.

AD – I love eating rice pudding when it's still warm; that's when it tastes its best. And if there's any leftover, I let it harden in the refrigerator and toast it in a frying pan until it's crispy. Heavenly!

PN – This dessert has a lot of carbohydrates. Make it on a weekend when you're doing a lot of physical activity. Your crispy rice doesn't sound too bad, chef. I'll have to try it.

HAZELNUT SPREAD

MAKES ABOUT 400 GRAMS - 14 OUNCES
PREPARATION TIME: 20 MINUTES
COOK TIME: 15 MINUTES

55 grams - 2 ounces / 3/8 cup hazelnuts
65 grams - 2 1/4 ounces dark chocolate (70 percent cocoa)
55 grams - 2 ounces milk chocolate
1 tablespoon honey
1/2 vanilla bean
200 grams - 2/3 cup evaporated milk

Make the hazelnut spread
Preheat the oven to 180°C - 350°F (gas mark 4). Spread the hazelnuts on a baking sheet and roast until they turn dark, 10–15 minutes. Place in a blender and grind to a paste. Transfer the paste to a bowl.

Prepare the chocolate
Chop up both chocolates. Set aside in another bowl.

Make the spread
Put 2 tablespoons water and the honey in a small saucepan. Split the vanilla bean and scrape the seeds out into the pan. Bring to a boil. Add the evaporated milk and mix well. Transfer to the blender and blend until very smooth. Then add the hazelnut paste, followed by the chocolate. Blend until very smooth.

Finish
Transfer the spread to a jar. Store at room temperature for up to 2 weeks.

AD - This spread is much cheaper to make than buying store-bought products. It can be made quickly and it tastes much better.

PN - Hooray! A spread that isn't packed full of fat and sugar, but instead with calcium, which is good for the bones of both young and old. Thank you, chef!

APPLES

CLEMENTINES

MANDARINS

MANGOS

ORANGES

PEARS

PINEAPPLE

BEETROOT

CABBAGE

CARROTS

CELERY

ENDIVE

GARLIC

JERUSALEM

ARTICHOKES

LEEKS

MACHE

MUSHROOMS

ONIONS

PARSNIPS

POTATOES

SALSIFY

SHALLOTS

SPINACH

SQUASH

TURNIPS

WINTER

SHALLOT VINAIGRETTE

MAKES: 20 CL - 2/3 CUP
PREPARATION TIME: 5 MINUTES
COOK TIME: 20 MINUTES

5 olive shallots (or regular shallots)
100 milliliter - 1/3 cup plus 1 tablespoon sherry vinegar
100 milliliter - 1/3 cup plus 1 tablespoon olive oil

Prepare the shallots
Peel and mince the shallots.

Make the shallot vinaigrette
Put the shallots in a small saucepan and add the vinegar. Simmer until the vinegar almost completely evaporates, about 20 minutes, stirring from time to time. Off the heat, gradually add the oil while whisking to thoroughly emulsify.

Finish
Transfer the vinaigrette to a bowl and let cool. Keep it refrigerated until serving time.

AD - This vinaigrette is the absolute best. Its strong flavor enhances that of asparagus and other vegetables.

PN - Like onion and garlic, the shallot is a natural health food, thanks to its high mineral and antioxidant content. Don't think twice about using this vinaigrette; it will do you the world of good.

GREEN CABBAGE BROTH

<u>SERVES 4</u>
PREPARATION TIME: 15 MINUTES
COOK TIME: 50 MINUTES

1 large green cabbage
Salt
Vinegar
4 carrots
4 celery stalks
1 white onion
1 clove
4 small leeks
150 grams - 5 1/2 ounces smoked bacon
1 liter - 4 1/4 cups pot-au-feu broth
(see p. 162) or poule au pot broth
(see p. 62), or 2 tablespoons white
miso paste diluted in 1 liter - 4
1/4 cups water
3 juniper berries
1 bay leaf
Freshly ground pepper

Prepare the cabbage
Cut the cabbage into six pieces, but keep the leaves attached to the stem. Wash in a bowl of water with some added vinegar. Bring lightly salted water to a boil in a saucepan. Immerse in the boiling water for 5 minutes, then drain in a colander and refresh immediately under very cold running water.

Prepare the other vegetables and the bacon
Peel and wash the carrots. Wash the celery stalks and remove the strings. Peel the onion and stud with the clove. Fill the sink with cold water. Cut off the tough green leaves from the leeks, make a few lengthwise incisions with a knife, and wash them in the sink. Drain. Cut the smoked bacon into lardons.

AD - If you don't have chicken or pot-au-feu broth, make this dish with miso. Since discovering this soybean paste in Japan thirty years ago, I always keep some in my fridge.

PN - Cabbage is a really good vegetable, filled with protective molecules. In countries where cabbage is part of the staple diet, there are lower rates of cancer and cardiovascular diseases.

Make the green cabbage broth
Combine all the vegetables in a cast-iron pot or Dutch oven. Pack them in well. Barely cover the vegetables with the broth, then add the juniper berries and bay leaf.

Cover the pan with its lid, bring to a boil, and simmer over medium heat for 30 minutes. Add the lardons and cook for 15 minutes more.

Check that the vegetables are cooked through with the tip of a knife.

Finish and serve
Check the flavor of the broth and adjust the seasoning with salt and pepper. Use a skimmer to take out the vegetables and bacon from the pan and arrange them among 4 soup plates. Pour the broth into a tureen or serving bowl and pass separately. Serve immediately, while very hot.

CARROT, ORANGE, AND ENDIVE SOUP

SERVES 4
PREPARATION TIME: 20 MINUTES
COOK TIME: 30 MINUTES

1 onion
1 kg - 2 pounds 4 ounces organic carrots
2 oranges
1 tablespoon olive oil
1 sprig thyme
1 teaspoon ground cumin
Salt
1 head endive (chicory)
1/2 bunch chervil
1/2 bunch flat-leaf parsley
Freshly ground pepper

AD - Carrot and orange is always a good combination. The orange adds a hint of acidity to the carrot, which is quite sweet. And the raw endive gives a hint of bitterness. It's a good marriage.

PN - If your soup turns out too thick, dilute it with orange juice. This will provide additional, fresh vitamin C. I really like the vegetable chiffonade because you have to chew this soup, which will make it even more satisfying.

Prepare the vegetables and oranges
Peel and mince the onion. Wash and dry the carrots. Set one aside and finely chop the others. Peel the oranges and separate the sections (segments).

Cook the soup
Heat the olive oil in a cast-iron pot or Dutch oven and cook the onion, over low heat, until translucent. Add the carrot pieces, orange sections, thyme, and cumin. Stir. Add 1 liter - 4 1/4 cups water. Lightly season with salt and stir again. Cook until the carrots are very soft, about 30 minutes.

Prepare the vegetable chiffonade
While the soup is cooking, wash the endive, cut off the base, and remove any outer leaves if necessary. Cut it into fine strips (chiffonade) and set aside in a bowl. Cut the reserved carrot into fine strips. Add them to the bowl. Wash, dry, and pluck the chervil and parsley and add them to the bowl. Toss thoroughly.

Finish and serve
Heat four bowls. Remove the thyme from the soup. Use a handheld immersion blender to blend the soup until smooth. Check and adjust the seasoning with salt and pepper. Transfer the soup to a tureen.

Place a handful of the vegetable chiffonade in each of 4 bowls, and pour the soup over the vegetables at the table.

Lentils are the seeds from a pod produced by an annual herbaceous plant. It is considered to be the world's oldest vegetable. Evidence of its existence has been discovered in Syrian excavations dating back 10,000 years, and its fame dates back to Jacob, a figure from the Bible and Koran, who sold his birthright to his brother Esau for a bowl of lentil stew. Grown throughout the Middle East since antiquity, lentils later spread to Europe and all over the planet. Long considered a humble food for peasants, and for a long time confined to rustic dishes, lentils have now been raised to the heights of gastronomy.

⬤ VARIETIES AND SEASONS

Lentils are categorized according to their color. The blond lentil is the largest and the variety that is most popular. Brown lentils are typically canned. Coral or pink lentils, cultivated in India, the Middle East, and North Africa, have a slightly peppery flavor. Red lentils are quite rare. Smooth and round black beluga lentils are grown in Canada. Green lentils are the most widely grown variety. Puy lentils have PDO status, while Berry lentils are covered by a protected geographical indication (PGI). Dried lentils are available year-round.

⬤ CHOOSING AND STORAGE

You should choose French lentils over imported ones (Canada, India, Nepal, China, and Turkey are the world's largest producers). Puy and Berry green lentils are quite easy to find. The blond lentils grown at Saint-Four, which are considered an outstanding product by Slow Food France, can be bought online. Only available as an import, coral or pink lentils are also available produced organically. All lentils should be stored in a dry place.

⬤ NUTRITION

Lentils are a popular staple among vegetarians because they are so full of proteins, minerals (including a fair amount of iron), and B-group vitamins. They are also an excellent source of complex carbohydrates and dietary fiber, and have a great ability to satiate.

⬤ USES AND COMBINATIONS

Lentils do not need to be soaked before cooking. They should always be cooked in unsalted cold water, and cooking can take between 5 minutes (for the pink variety) and 30-40 minutes for other varieties. Salt is added at the end of the cooking process. Lentils feature in a large number of Asian dishes, and in French cuisine they are traditionally combined with salted pork and sausages, and also with foie gras and pigeon.

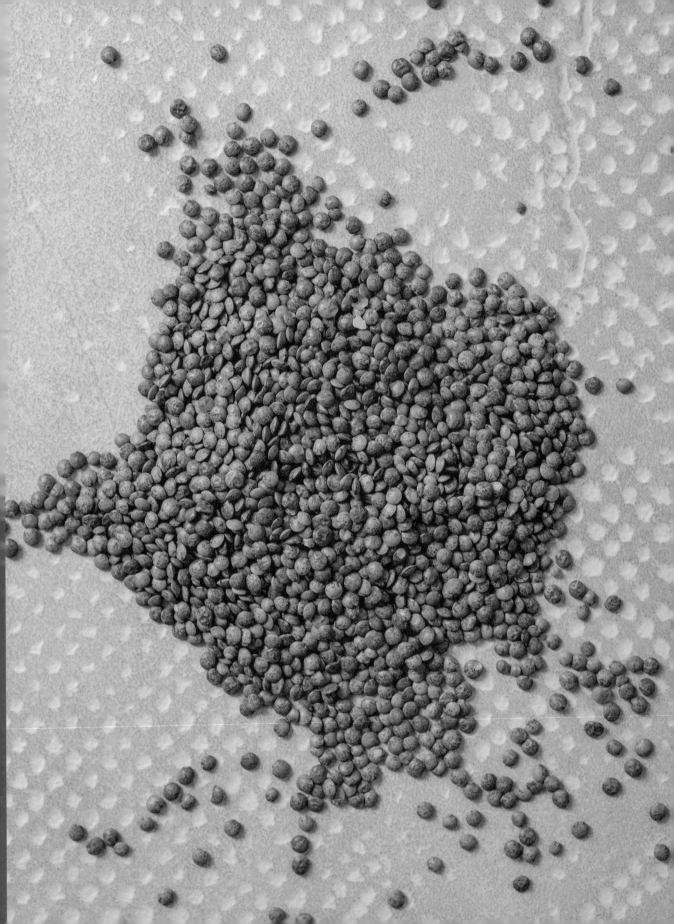

LENTIL SOUP WITH RICOTTA

200 grams - 7 ounces/1 cup green lentils
1 carrot
2 shallots
1 onion
1 clove
1/2 bunch flat-leaf parsley
2 cloves garlic
150 g - 5 1/2 ounces smoked side (streaky) bacon
1 liter - 4 1/4 cups chicken broth (see p. 62)
1 sprig thyme
1 bay leaf
Salt
Freshly ground pepper
2 tablespoons pistachios, shelled
150 grams - 5 1/2 ounces/2/3 cup ricotta cheese
1 tablespoon olive oil
100 milliliters - 1/3 cup plus 1 tablespoon light (single) cream
1 organic, unwaxed lemon

AD - Like beans, lentils should only be salted at the end of the cooking process, otherwise their skin turns hard. You can easily make this soup with other legumes, such as chickpeas or beans.

PN - What a blessing lentils are! They are a source of vegetable protein, complex carbohydrates, dietary fiber, and lots of minerals, including plenty of iron. And they have very few calories. This soup is particularly beneficial, while being light and filling at the same time.

Make the soup
Rinse the lentils. Wash, peel, and finely chop the carrot. Peel and mince the shallots. Peel the onion and stud with the clove. Rinse and pluck the parsley leaves. Cut the stems into small pieces.

In a cast-iron pot or Dutch oven, combine the lentils, carrot, shallots, parsley stems, studded onion, unpeeled garlic, and smoked bacon. Add the broth and bring to a boil. Then add the thyme and bay leaf, and cook for 30 minutes, skimming regularly.

Season with salt and pepper only after cooking for 20 minutes.

Prepare the ricotta with parsley
Finely chop the pistachios, mince the parsley leaves, and combine in a bowl. Add the cheese and olive oil. Season with salt and pepper and mix. Set aside in the refrigerator.

Finish
Remove the onion, thyme, bay leaf, garlic cloves, and bacon from the pan. Dice the bacon to make lardons. Heat a dry frying pan and cook them well. Use a handheld immersion blender to blend the lentils until smooth, then add the cream and blend again briefly. Adjust the seasoning.

Serve
Pour the soup into a tureen and add the lardons. Use two teaspoons to shape the ricotta mixture into quenelles and arrange them in 4 serving bowls. Grate lemon zest over them. Pour the soup into each bowl at the table.

VELOUTÉ OF JERUSALEM ARTICHOKE WITH COFFEE

SERVES 4
PREPARATION TIME: 25 MINUTES
COOK TIME: 30 MINUTES

15 large Jerusalem artichokes
Juice of 1 lemon
1 white onion
Olive oil
500 milliliters - 2 cups
lowfat (2%) milk
4 teaspoons finely and
freshly ground coffee
Salt
Freshly ground pepper
4 chives

Prepare the Jerusalem artichokes
Peel and slice the Jerusalem artichokes. Put them in water to which the lemon juice has been added to keep them from turning black. Then drain and immerse in a saucepan filled with cold water. Place over the heat and boil for 8 minutes.

Make the velouté
Peel and finely slice the onion. Heat a little olive oil in a saucepan and sweat the onion over medium heat without browning it. Drain the Jerusalem artichokes and add to the pan. Stir and cook for 5 minutes. Add the milk and 2 teaspoons ground coffee, season with salt and pepper, and stir. Cook until the Jerusalem artichokes are very soft, about 20 minutes.

Blend with a handheld immersion blender until perfectly smooth. Place a conical strainer over another saucepan and strain the velouté.

Finish and serve
Reheat the velouté in the saucepan over low heat. Check and adjust the seasoning. Rinse, dry, and finely chop the chives. Sprinkle the velouté with the remaining ground coffee and chopped chives. Serve very hot.

AD - Large Jerusalem artichokes are easier to peel than small ones. You need a small knife (not a vegetable peeler) because their skin is thick and tough.

PN - Jerusalem artichokes contain a lot of dietary fiber and inulin, a carbohydrate we aren't able to metabolize. That's why they aren't always easy to digest, which causes flatulence. But here, with a long blanching process, well-cooked, and well-blended, these Jerusalem artichokes won't cause any problems.

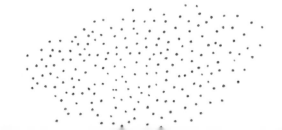

CREAM OF PUMPKIN SOUP WITH CHESTNUTS

SERVES 4
PREPARATION TIME: 10 MINUTES
COOK TIME: 25 MINUTES

1 pumpkin (winter squash),
about 1.8 kilograms - 4
pounds
1 slice smoked bacon, about
10 grams - 3 1/2 ounces
Olive oil
Salt
1 liter - 4 1/4 cups *lait
ribot* or buttermilk
1 clove garlic
1/4 bunch flat-leaf parsley
300 grams - 10 1/2 ounces
cooked chestnuts (from a jar
or vacuum-packed)
Freshly ground pepper
3 grams - 1 1/2 teaspoons
ground cardamom

AD - If you feel like using raw chestnuts, put them on a baking sheet and roast in the oven at 200°C - 400°F (gas mark 6) for 40-50 minutes. Then put on a pair of gloves so that you can peel them without burning yourself.

PN - This soup is very nourishing. It's quite good. Follow it up with a soft-boiled egg with toast soldiers, a salad, a piece of cheese, and a piece of fruit. And there you have a very balanced dinner.

Prepare the pumpkin
Cut the pumpkin into several sections, then peel them with a large, very sharp knife. Remove any seeds and cut the flesh into a small dice.

Make the cream of pumpkin
Brown the bacon in a cast-iron pot or Dutch oven with a little olive oil until browned. Add the diced pumpkin, season with salt, and sweat for 10 minutes while stirring constantly.

Add the laid ribot or buttermilk and unpeeled garlic clove, and cook over low heat for 10 minutes.
Remove the skin from the garlic clove. Use a handheld immersion blender to blend the soup until it is very smooth.

Prepare the parsley and chestnuts
Rinse, dry, pluck, and finely chop the parsley leaves.
Halve the chestnuts. Heat a little olive oil in a saucepan and sweat them for about 5 minutes. Transfer to a dish and keep warm.

Finish and serve
Check the temperature and seasoning of the soup, adding pepper and more salt, if needed. Add the cardamom and stir.

Divide the chestnuts among 4 bowls and sprinkle with the chopped parsley. Pour the cream of pumpkin soup over them. Serve immediately.

MARINATED TURNIPS

SERVES 4
PREPARATION TIME: 30 MINUTES
COOK TIME: 1 MINUTE
REST TIME: 20 MINUTES
CHILL TIME: 1 HOUR

400 grams - 14 ounces baby turnips, with greens (tops)
Salt
100 milliliter - 1/3 cup plus 1 tablespoons white wine vinegar
1 tablespoon honey
4 tablespoons olive oil
5 tablespoons tosazu sauce (dashi vinegar)
3-centimeter- - 1 1/4-inch-length ginger

Prepare the turnips
Peel, wash, and dry the turnips. Select a few pretty turnip greens and finely chop them. Use a mandoline with safety guard to finely slice the turnips. Transfer to a mixing bowl. Season with salt, mix, and leave the turnips to release their residual water, 15–20 minutes.

Make the marinated turnips
Pour the vinegar into a saucepan and add the same volume in water, along with the honey and 2 pinches of salt. Bring to a boil.

Drain the turnips in a strainer, then add to the pan. Cook for only 1 minute after the liquid comes back to a boil. Remove the pan from the heat and let cool. Finally, add the olive oil, tosazu sauce, and chopped turnip greens.

Finish
Peel and chop the ginger. Add to the pan with the turnips and mix. Transfer the contents of the pan to a bowl and marinate in the refrigerator for 1 hour.

Serve
Spread out the marinated turnips in a dish, or serve on 4 plates. Serve very cold.

AD - My favorite variety of turnip is Tokyo Cross, which has a very delicate bitterness. If you find it, don't hesitate to buy it.

PN - Like other members of the mustard family, turnips contain molecules that protect against cancer. This is one of their best qualities. They also contain plentiful minerals and, particularly, dietary fiber, which can make them a little difficult to digest. Chew them well.

QUINOA, AVOCADO, AND ORANGE

SERVES 4
PREPARATION TIME: 5 MINUTES
COOK TIME: 15 MINUTES

300 grams - 10 1/2 ounces/1
3/4 cups quinoa
2 organic, unwaxed oranges
1 avocado
1 lemon
1 medium white onion
5 sprigs flat-leaf parsley
2 tablespoons olive oil
Salt
Freshly ground pepper

AD - Quinoa is easily found at organic food stores. I love this grain.

PN - Quinoa makes everybody—even
those who believe they are gluten
intolerant—happy. Quinoa isn't a cereal.
It's the seeds from a herbaceous plant,
from the same botanical family as
beets and spinach.

Prepare the quinoa

Put the quinoa in a sieve and rinse in plenty of running water. Put in a saucepan and add a little more than double its volume in water (about 750 milliliters - 3 cups). Bring to a boil and cook over medium heat for 15 minutes. Let cool.

Prepare the orange, avocado, and onion

In the meantime, supreme 1 orange, separating the individual sections (segments) over a bowl to collect the juice. Set aside the sections on a plate. Halve the avocado, remove the seed, scoop out the flesh, and cut into cubes. Put the cubes of avocado in a bowl as they are cut. Squeeze the lemon over the cubed avocado and gently mix. Peel and slice the onion into rounds. Add to the bowl with the avocado.

Make the orange and parsley vinaigrette

Rinse, dry, and pluck the parsley leaves. Set aside a few leaves for serving and chop the rest. Put the chopped parsley in the bowl with the orange juice.

Grate the zest of the second orange into a bowl and set aside. Squeeze the orange over the bowl with the orange juice and parsley. Add the olive oil and whisk. Add the orange zest into the bowl and whisk again.

Finish and serve

Transfer the quinoa to a bowl. Add the avocado, onion, and orange and parsley vinaigrette, then mix gently so as not to crush the avocado. Adjust the seasoning with salt and pepper.

Arrange the orange sections over the top, sprinkle with the reserved parsley leaves, and serve.

SHRIMP TARTARE

400 grams - 14 ounces live pink shrimp
2 tablespoons fresh dulse
2 tablespoons fresh sea lettuce
3 tablespoons white sesame seeds
1 oyster
2 tablespoons sesame oil
2 tablespoons olive oil
1 teaspoon soy sauce
1 teaspoon rice vinegar
Salt
1 pinch Espelette pepper
1 loaf rye bread

AD – What about the shrimp heads, you say? That's easy. Heat a little olive oil in a frying pan, throw in the heads, and cook them for 4-5 minutes with a crushed garlic clove until they are crispy. They make an ideal snack to serve with drinks.

PN – Given the price of pink shrimp, it's nice of you to give us a recipe so that the heads don't go to waste. This tartar is invigorating, with all the mineral-rich dulse and sea lettuce seaweeds.

Prepare the shrimp
Cut the heads off the shrimp and reserve for another use. Peel and coarsely chop the bodies with a large knife. Transfer to a bowl and refrigerate.

Put the dulse and sea lettuce in a bowl filled with water. Shake them well, then drain. Repeat this desalting process one more time. Chop them up with a knife and set aside in the bowl with the shrimp.

Make the sesame condiment
Heat a dry nonstick frying pan and toast the sesame seeds until light golden.

Set aside 1 tablespoon of the seeds on a plate. Transfer the rest to a mortar and pound to the consistency of a paste.

Place a small strainer over a bowl and shuck the oyster over it. Add the oyster flesh and strained liquor to the mortar and pound until well incorporated. Add 1 tablespoon of the sesame oil, mix well, and refrigerate.

Make the shrimp tartare
To the bowl with the chopped shrimp and seaweed, add the reserved sesame seeds, the remaining sesame oil, and the olive oil, soy sauce, rice vinegar, and a pinch of salt and Espelette pepper.

Mix very gently, then refrigerate until it is time to serve.

Prepare the toasts
Cut the rye bread into very thin slices. Toast them quickly, taking care not to let them burn.

Finish and serve
Serve the shrimp tartare and sesame condiment on plates. Arrange the toasts around them and serve.

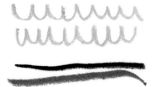

KALE AND HAKE WITH BROTH

2 hake fillets, skin on, about 700
grams - 1 pound 9 ounces
20 grams - 1 1/2 tablespoons butter
1/4 head Savoy cabbage
2 large white mushrooms
1 carrot
1 stalk celery
1 onion
1 leek
1 clove garlic
4 juniper berries
4 black peppercorns
120 grams - 4 1/4 ounces smoked
haddock
1 head radicchio di Treviso
8 kale leaves
Salt
Freshly ground pepper
Olive oil

AD - Radicchio di Treviso is an Italian chicory. There are different varieties. If you can't find this particular type, replace with a radicchio heart.

PN - And if you can't find kale, Savoy cabbage can replace both the radicchio and kale.

Prepare the hake fillets
Ask your fishmonger to fillet the hake. Carefully remove all of the bones. Mash the butter with a fork until it has softened, then spread it over the skin side of the fillets. Set aside.

Make the broth
Separate the cabbage leaves, finely slice them, and put them in a cast-iron pot or Dutch oven. Cut the stems off the mushrooms and wash and finely slice the caps. Add them to the pan. Peel the carrot, remove the tough strings from the celery stalk, peel the onion, and trim the leek. Finely slice the carrot, celery, and onion and add to the pan. Cut rounds from the white of the leek, reserving 4, and add to the pan, along with the garlic clove, juniper berries, and peppercorns. Cover with water. Bring to a boil without adding salt, then lower the heat and simmer for 30 minutes. Cut the haddock into pieces and add. Remove the pan from the heat and poach the haddock for 10 minutes. Remove the haddock and set aside on a plate. Place a fine conical strainer over a saucepan and strain the broth without pressing so that it remains clear.

Prepare the vegetable garnish
Separate, wash, dry, and set aside the radicchio and kale leaves.

Cook the kale and fish
Put the buttered hake fillets into a frying pan, skin-side down, with the kale leaves and add a ladle of broth. Bring to a boil, turn off the heat, and cover the pan with a lid. Braise for 5 minutes.

Finish and serve
Line 4 heated bowls with the braised kale. Halve the hake fillets and place one half into each bowl, surrounded by the radicchio leaves, raw leek rounds, and haddock pieces. Season with salt and pepper. Add the cooking liquid from the hake to the pan with the broth and reheat. Add a little olive oil and transfer to a pitcher. Serve separately.

CAULIFLOWER, EGGS, AND HERBS

SERVES 4
PREPARATION TIME: 10 MINUTES
COOK TIME: 20 MINUTES
REST TIME: 10 MINUTES

1 large cauliflower
Wine Vinegar
Salt
4 eggs
6 sprigs flat-leaf parsley
1 white onion
2 slices whole-wheat bread
1 preserved lemon (see p. 200)
4 tablespoons olive oil, plus more for the pan
5 grams - 1 teaspoon butter
2 tablespoons red wine vinegar
Freshly ground pepper

Prepare the cauliflower
Remove the leaves from the cauliflower and cut the stem flush with the florets. Put the cauliflower in a large bowl, cover with water, add a good splash of vinegar, and soak for 10 minutes. Drain.

Boil 1.5 L - 6 cups salted water in a pot and carefully add the cauliflower; cook for about 20 minutes. Check that it is cooked through with the tip of a knife; it should be tender but still firm.

Prepare the hard-boiled eggs and herbs
In the meantime, hard boil the eggs (9 minutes) in boiling water. Cool and peel the eggs. Quarter the eggs and set aside on a plate. Rinse, dry, pluck, and chop the parsley leaves. Peel the onion and slice into thin rounds. Set each ingredient aside separately in a bowl.

Make the croutons
Toast the bread, then break it up into small croutons.

Finish
Slice the preserved lemon rind into small pieces. Drain the cauliflower, let cool slightly, then separate the florets. Heat a little olive oil and the butter in a frying pan. Sauté the florets to color, then arrange them in a bowl to more or less reproduce the shape of a whole cauliflower, or divide among individual plates.

Add the hard-boiled egg quarters, parsley, onion rounds, croutons, and preserved lemon rind. Drizzle with vinegar and the 4 tablespoons olive oil. Season with a turn of the pepper mill and serve.

AD - This dish is a classic of French cuisine. The great Escoffier named it "cauliflower Polonaise." We replace the beurre noisette with olive oil, which is healthier.

PN - This dish is a festival of antioxidants thanks to the cauliflower, onion, and parsley, which are filled with them. With the hard-boiled eggs and their protein, what you have is a good one-dish meal.

SCALLOP CARPACCIO, BLACK RADISH, AND PEANUTS

2 tablespoons unsalted peanuts
12 great (king) scallops
1 tablespoon olive oil
2 organic, unwaxed limes
1 teaspoon soy sauce
4 white mushrooms
1 small black radish
1 tray (punnet) shiso shoots

AD - Store the rest of the peanut condiment in the refrigerator. You can use it to season vegetables or on a simply fried or steamed fillet of fish. The rest of the black radish can go into a soup. It shouldn't be thrown away.

PN - Peanuts are the source of the oil of the same name. They are sources of dietary fiber, good unsaturated fat, and, on the whole, are good for your health, although they should be eaten in moderation given their fat content.

Make the peanut condiment
Heat a dry nonstick frying pan and toast the peanuts until light golden. Transfer to a mortar and pound to the consistency of a paste. Add 1 tablespoon hot water and mix until incorporated. Refrigerate.

Prepare the scallops
Rinse them under running water and remove their membranes. Slice each scallop across the middle into two or three disks. Spread them out over a dish.

In a bowl, mix together the olive oil, the juice of 1 lime, and the soy sauce. Brush the scallop slices generously with this marinade. Cover the dish with plastic wrap (cling film) and refrigerate. Set aside the rest of the marinade.

Prepare the mushrooms and black radish
Clean the mushrooms and cut off their stems (save them for a soup). Use a mandoline with safety guard to cut the caps into 8 thin slices each (24 in total), spread them out over a dish, and rub with lemon in batches.

Use a new scouring sponge to scrub the radish under running water. Rinse well. Use a mandoline with safety guard to cut about 20 thin slices. Add to the bowl with the remaining marinade.

Finish and serve
Chill 4 plates in the refrigerator or freezer. Rinse and shake dry the shiso shoots. Arrange mushroom and scallop slices and peanut condiment on the plates. Cover with the marinade with radish slices, grate a little lime zest over the top, and decorate with shiso shoots. Serve very cold.

SAUERKRAUT AND SALMON

800 grams - 12 1/4 ounces/3 1/2 cups cooked sauerkraut
1 (400-gram - 14-ounce) organic salmon fillet
1 handful hay
2 onions
2 apples
15 grams - 1/2 ounce/1 tablespoon goose fat
4-5 juniper berries
1 (750-milliliters) bottle Riesling wine
1 egg yolk
200 milliliter - 3/4 cup plus 1 tablespoon buttermilk
Salt
Freshly ground pepper
1 bunch dill
Bottarga for grating

AD - Taste the sauerkraut before rinsing. If its flavor isn't very strong, it is not necessary to rinse it. Hay is easily found, packed in bags, online.

PN - This dish is so light. Sauerkraut has very few calories. It is much easier to digest than cabbage because it's fermented, but it contains just as many protective compounds of all kinds.

Prepare the sauerkraut
Put the sauerkraut in a large bowl filled with water to rinse. Drain and squeeze with your hands to remove the water. Place on a clean cloth and toss it a few times to aerate.

Prepare the fish
Cut the salmon fillet into four 100-gram - 3 1/2-ounce pieces and place on a small wire rack. Put the hay in a cast-iron pan and light it with a chef's torch. Place the rack with the salmon steaks in the pan and immediately cover with a lid to put out the flames. Smoke the salmon for 10 minutes.

Make the sauerkraut mixture
Peel and finely slice the onions. Peel, halve, and core the apples, and cut each half in three pieces.

Melt the goose fat in a cast-iron pan, then sweat the onion slices and apple pieces for 3 minutes while stirring; do not brown. Add the juniper berries, sauerkraut, and smoked salmon steaks. Pour in the wine, bring to a boil, and cover the pan.

Cook for about 10 minutes over very low heat, then take out the salmon steaks. They should be hot but very pink inside. Transfer them to a dish and keep warm.

Dilute the egg yolk with the buttermilk in a bowl and add to the pan with the sauerkraut. Stir until the sauerkraut is well-bound. Season with salt and pepper.

Finish and serve
Rinse, dry, pluck, and mince the dill tips. Add to the sauerkraut and mix. Put the sauerkraut in a dish. Arrange the salmon steaks on top, grate bottarga over all, and serve.

CORN PANCAKES, SALMON ROE, DILL, AND MACHE

SERVES 4
PREPARATION TIME: 20
MINUTES
COOK TIME: 15 MINUTES

1 (300-gram - 10 1/2-ounce can) corn kernels (about 1 3/4 cups drained)
150 grams - 1/2 cup heavy (double) cream
2 eggs
1 tablespoon flour
50 grams - 1/2 cup grated Gruyère cheese
Salt
Freshly ground pepper
1 bunch dill
1 organic, unwaxed lemon
200 grams - 7 ounces mache (lamb's lettuce or corn salad)
Olive oil
1 bunch chives
1 tablespoon cider vinegar
1 small jar salmon roe

AD - I love that this dish is both rustic and sophisticated, and the contrast between the hot pancakes and the cold dill cream and mâche.

PN - This one-dish meal is perfect for dinner. It is high in carbohydrates, which should help you sleep well. And mache is a real nutritional miracle; you should never be without it.

Make the corn pancake batter
Empty the can of corn kernels into a strainer and drain well. Put half of the corn in the bowl of a food processor and blend to a smooth paste. Transfer to a mixing bowl. Add half of the cream (75 grams - 1/4 cup), the eggs, the flour, the rest of the corn, and the grated Gruyère. Mix and lightly season with salt and pepper.

Make the dill cream
Rinse dry, pluck, and mince the dill tips. Put the rest of the cream (75 grams - 1/4 cup) in a bowl and whisk until very foamy. Zest the lemon; set the zest aside. Squeeze the lemon into the cream. Mix gently, then add the dill. Refrigerate.

Prepare the corn salad
Wash, dry, and pluck the mâche leaves.

Cook the corn pancakes
Preheat the oven to 180°C - 350°F (gas mark 4). Lightly brush a frying pan with oil. Pour in a quarter of the batter and tilt the pan in all directions to spread it well. Cook for 2-3 minutes. Check that the bottom is golden by lifting the pancake with a spatula (turner), turn it over, and cook the other side the same way. Make another 3 pancakes, transfer to a dish, and keep them warm in the oven.

Finish and serve
Rinse and dry the chives. Cut them into 3-centimeter - 1 1/4-inch lengths. Put the mache in a bowl, dress with the cider vinegar and 2 tablespoons olive oil, and season with salt and pepper
Serve the pancakes on a serving dish or on individual plates. Put a heaping tablespoon dill cream on each one. Use a small spoon to top with salmon roe, and add the chives. Add a little of the grated lemon zest. Serve the dressed mache in piles around the pancakes and serve immediately.

CRAB CROQUETTES AND SPICY AVOCADO WITH PASSION FRUIT

6 slices sandwich bread
12-15 cooked crab claws
5 sprigs cilantro (coriander)
2-centimeter- - 3/4-inch-length ginger
2 eggs
1 tablespoon heavy (double) cream
8 tablespoons olive oil
2 organic, unwaxed lemons
3 avocados
Salt
Cayenne pepper
2 scallions
2 passion fruits

AD - Don't be tempted to use canned crab meat. The meat will be wet and your croquettes will fall apart. Take the time to crack open the claws and take out the meat. Get your children or friends to help you.

PN - Here's a wonderful one-dish meal, with protein from the crab meat, carbohydrates from the bread crumbs and onion, dietary fiber from the avocado, and rich in vitamins and minerals.

Make the fresh bread crumbs
Cut the bread into small pieces. Put the pieces in a food processor and grind into crumbs. Transfer to a plate.

Prepare the crab croquettes
Crack the crab claws and remove the meat. You should have about 250 grams - 9 ounces in total.

Pluck and mince the cilantro. Peel and grate the ginger. Break the eggs into a bowl. Add the cream, 4 tablespoons of the olive oil, and the cilantro and ginger. Mix. Zest, then squeeze one lemon; add the zest and juice to the bowl. Mix, then add the crab meat. Continue to mix until smooth.

Shape the mixture into small croquettes and coat them in the bread crumbs as they are made. Transfer to a baking dish and refrigerate until they are very firm, about 1 hour but not until they are firm.

Make the spicy avocado
In the meantime, halve the avocados and remove their seeds. Use a teaspoon to scoop out their flesh and transfer to a food processor. Add the juice of the second lemon, some salt, and a pinch of cayenne pepper. Blend until smooth. Transfer to a bowl.

Peel and mince the onions and add to the bowl. Cut open the passion fruits, scoop out their seeds and juice, and add to the bowl. Mix gently and refrigerate until it's cool.

Finish and serve
Preheat the oven to 180°C - 350°F (gas mark 4). Put the dish with the croquettes in the oven and cook for 12 minutes. Let cool a little, then arrange them on plates. Put a serving of spicy avocado next to the croquettes and serve.

GNOCCHI WITH SEAWEED, BOTTARGA, AND SALMON ROE

Coarse salt
4 large potatoes
1 tablespoon flour, plus more for dusting
1 egg
Salt
Freshly ground pepper
2 tablespoons fresh sea lettuce
2 tablespoons red dulse
2 tablespoons wakame seaweed
1 lettuce heart
Olive oil
1 tablespoon mirin
1 tablespoon sake
20 grams - 4 teaspoons bottarga
1 small jar salmon roe
2 tablespoons dried nori slivers

AD - It takes time to make gnocchi, but they're really delicious. Having said that, you can make them a day ahead and finish cooking them on the day you're serving the dish. Refrigerate them in an airtight container.

PN - Bottarga and salmon roe for animal protein, potatoes and seaweed for plant protein. This dish has no shortage of protein. There is no need for meat or fish in this meal, but a dairy product such as cheese would round it off nicely.

Prepare the potatoes for the gnocchi

Preheat the oven to 200°C - 400°F (gas mark 6). Cover a baking sheet with coarse salt, put the potatoes on the bed of salt, cover with aluminum foil, and bake for 1 hour 30 minutes. Check that they are cooked through using the tip of a knife; it should pierce the potatoes easily. Peel and mash the potatoes, then press the mash through a drum sieve. Mix with the flour and egg. Season with salt and pepper. Roll into a ball.

Make the gnocchi

Dust the work surface with flour. Cut the ball into four pieces and roll out each piece into a long strip. Cut a piece every 2 cm - 3/4 inch. Roll each piece into a ball and press against the back of a fork to create a ridged pattern. Set aside on a tray covered with flour.

Prepare the seaweed and lettuce

Immerse the sea lettuce, dulse, and wakame in a bowl filled with water and shake them. Drain and repeat the process. Pat dry and coarsely chop with a knife. Transfer to a bowl and set aside. Pluck the small yellow leaves from the lettuce heart (save the rest for a salad). Wash and set aside.

Cook the gnocchi

Immerse the gnocchi in a saucepan filled with boiling salted water. Remove the gnocchi with a slotted spoon once they have floated to the surface. Heat a little olive oil in a frying pan and add 3 tablespoons of the gnocchi cooking water. Add the gnocchi and cook for 5 minutes. Add the chopped seaweed, the lettuce leaves, the mirin, and sake, and toss.

Finish and serve

Cut the bottarga into thin slices. Serve the gnocchi on a serving dish or on individual plates. Scatter with slices of bottarga, salmon roe, and nori slivers. Serve immediately.

POT-AU-FEU

SERVES 6-8
PREPARATION TIME: 30 MINUTES
COOK TIME: 3 HOURS 30 MINUTES
REST TIME: 30 MINUTES

2 marrow bones
500 grams - 1 pound 2 ounces fatty cut of beef (plate/brisket)
500 grams - 1 pound 2 ounces lean cut of beef (neck)
500 grams - 1 pound 2 ounces gelatinous cut of beef (flank steak)
1 oxtail
8 medium leeks
8 medium carrots
2 stalks celery
1 green cabbage
5 onions
4 cloves
4 stems flat-leaf parsley
2 sprigs thyme
1 bay leaf
2 cloves garlic, unpeeled
Salt
10 black peppercorns
Freshly ground pepper

AD - Actually, there isn't really a season for pot-au-feu. You can enjoy it just as much in fall as in spring. Serve it the classic way with mustard, coarse salt, and pickled cucumbers.

PN - There's a lot of meat in this dish. But that's okay, because you can use leftovers to make Shepherd's Pie later (see p. 153). Store the rest of the broth in the refrigerator or freezer; you'll make good use of it too.

Prepare the marrow bones and meat
Soak the marrow bones in a bowl filled with cold water for 30 minutes. Tie the pieces of beef plate, neck, and flank steak with kitchen twine. Cut the oxtail into large pieces.

Prepare the vegetables and bouquet garni
Peel the leeks. Cut off the tough green leaves and set aside. Make 2 incisions with a knife in the white part of the leek and wash carefully. Peel the carrots. Wash and remove the tough strings from the celery stalks. Quarter the cabbage. Peel the onions and stud 4 with one clove each. Make a bouquet garni by wrapping the parsley stems, thyme sprigs, and bay leaf with the leek leaves and tying with kitchen twine.

Cook the pot-au-feu
Put the different cuts of meat in a large cast-iron pot or Dutch oven. Cover with plenty of cold water and bring to a boil. Skim gently. When there is no more foam, add the vegetables, garlic cloves, and bouquet garni. Season with salt and add the peppercorns. Simmer for 3 hours 15 minutes. Soak the marrow bones in a bowl filled with cold water for 30 minutes. Drain the marrow bones, wrap in cheesecloth (muslin), and add them to the pot. Cook for 15 minutes more.

Finish and serve
Remove the meat from the pan, transfer to a heated dish and untie. Take the leeks, carrots, celery, and onions out of the pan and arrange around the meat. Take the marrow bones out of the pan, remove the cloth, and add to the dish. Strain the broth into a saucepan. Season with salt and pepper. Bring the broth back to a boil and pour into individual mugs (reserve the rest). Serve immediately.

SHEPHERD'S PIE WITH JERUSALEM ARTICHOKES

SERVES 4
PREPARATION TIME: 25 MINUTES
COOK TIME: 30 MINUTES

4 Agria potatoes
6 Jerusalem artichokes
Salt
2 red onions
1/2 bunch flat-leaf parsley
1 bunch chives
500 milliliters - 2 cups *lait ribot* or buttermilk
600 grams - 1 pound 5 ounces leftover meat from pot-au-feu (see p. 150)
50 grams - 1/3 cup capers, drained
100 milliliters - 1/3 cup plus 1 tablespoon sherry vinegar
Freshly ground pepper
1 hunk stale bread
50 grams - 2 ounces grated Parmesan cheese

AD - *Jerusalem artichokes really give mashed potatoes a different feel.*

PN - *And the onions, capers, and vinegar do the same to the filling. It makes my mouth water. I like this one-dish meal a lot. You can serve it with a salad.*

Prepare the vegetables
Wash and peel the potatoes and Jerusalem artichokes. Cut them into small pieces. Heat salted water in two saucepans. Cook the potatoes in one and the Jerusalem artichokes in the other until they soften, for approximately 20 min. You can check with a tip of a knife. In the meantime, peel and mince the onions. Rinse and dry the parsley and chives. Pluck the parsley leaves and mince together with the chives. Set aside. Drain the potatoes and Jerusalem artichokes, then mash together with a fork, or use a food mill. Transfer the mash to a saucepan and place over low heat. Gradually stir in the buttermilk. Season with salt.

Make the filling
Shred the leftover meat from the pot-au-feu and place in a large bowl. Add the minced onions and herbs, as well as the capers, and vinegar. Combine thoroughly. Season with salt and pepper.

Make the Parmesan bread crumbs
Break up the stale bread, put in a food processor, and grind into crumbs. Mix with the Parmesan.

Prepare the hachis Parmentier
Preheat the oven to 180°C - 350°F (gas mark 4). Spread a layer of the mashed potatoes and Jerusalem artichokes over the bottom of an ovenproof dish, followed by a layer of the meat mixture, and finally another layer of the mash. Sprinkle with an even coating of Parmesan bread crumbs.

Put the dish in the oven and cook until the cheese is melted and browned. Let the dish rest for 20 minutes before serving.

CHICKEN, ENDIVES, AND ALMONDS

5 sprigs cilantro (coriander)
5-centimeter- - 2-inch-length ginger
1 bird's-eye chili pepper
1 (150-gram - 5.3-ounce) container plain (natural) yogurt
2 tablespoons light (single) cream
1 pinch Espelette pepper
4 free-range chicken breasts, about 150g - 5 1/2 ounces each
Salt
8 heads endive
Olive oil
2 cloves garlic
1 pinch superfine (caster) sugar
50 grams - 2 ounces/1/3 cup golden raisins (sultanas)
1/4 bunch flat-leaf parsley
80 grams - 2 7/8 ounces/3/4 cup sliced (flaked) almonds
80 grams - 2 7/8 ounces/ 1 3/4 cups fresh bread crumbs
Freshly ground pepper

AD - If you can, use free-range chicken. It's a guarantee of quality

PN - One breast fillet per person is basically enough to fill your protein quota. The raisins tone down the bitterness of the endives; they're an extra.

Prepare the chicken a day ahead
Rinse, dry, and pluck the cilantro leaves. Peel the ginger, and remove the seeds from the chili pepper. Finely chop them and add to a bowl. Add the yogurt, cream, and Espelette pepper. Mix. Season the chicken breasts with salt and coat with the yogurt marinade. Wrap each breast in plastic wrap (cling film) and refrigerate for 24 hours.

On the day the dish is being served, prepare the endives
Preheat the oven to 180°C - 350°F (gas mark 4). Wash, dry, and halve the endives lengthwise. Discard the core. Pour 2 tablespoons olive oil in a baking dish and add the endive halves. Crush the garlic cloves and add to the endives. Season with salt and add a pinch of sugar. Bake in the oven for 15 minutes. Turn the endives and add 50 milliliters - 3 1/2 teaspoons of water and the raisins. Scrape with a flexible spatula (scraper) to deglaze the caramelized juices and then use a spoon to baste the endives with this liquid. Bake for 5 minutes more, basting one time. Remove the endives from the oven and lower the oven temperature to 210°C - 410°F (gas mark 6). Rinse, dry, pluck, and mince the parsley leaves. Add the parsley to the endive, cover with aluminum foil, and keep warm.

Cook the chicken
Mix the sliced almonds with the bread crumbs on a plate. Brush a baking dish with oil. Dredge the chicken breasts in the almond-bread crumb mixture and place in the oiled dish. Bake the chicken breasts in the oven for 10 minutes.

Finish and serve
Season the breasts with salt and pepper, arrange over the endives, and serve in the dish.

SALSIFY AND SCALLOPS

16 great (king) scallops
12 salsify roots
Juice of 1 lemon
Salt
3 juniper berries
30 grams - 1 ounce/2 tablespoons butter
100 milliliter - 1/3 cup plus 1 tablespoon chicken broth (see p. 62)
1 tablespoon balsamic vinegar
1 organic, unwaxed orange
2 sprigs basil
Olive oil
Freshly ground pepper

AD - What we typically know as salsify is in fact scorzonera or black salsify. White salsify is practically impossible to find, whereas the less fibrous black salsify is readily available in markets in winter.

PN - Part of the carbohydrate content of salsify is made up of inulin, which gives a slightly sweet flavor. But we don't have an enzyme with which to digest the inulin, which ferments in the digestive tract. This can cause indigestion.

Prepare the scallops
Clean the scallops under running water and carefully remove their membranes. Slice each scallop in half across the middle to make two disks. Transfer the disks to a plate, cover with plastic wrap (cling film), and refrigerate.

Prepare the salsify
Wash and peel the salsify roots and cut them into four lengths. As they are cut, set them in a bowl of water with the lemon juice. Drain and then cook the salsify in a pot of lightly salted boiling water for 20 minutes, then drain.

Cook the salsify
Crush and finely chop the juniper berries. Heat half of the butter (15 grams - 1 tablespoon) in a cast-iron pan. When it turns brown (*beurre noisette*), add half of the salsify and brown quickly. Add the chicken broth and balsamic vinegar, and cook until the salsify becomes very soft, about 10 minutes. In the meantime, heat the rest of the butter (15 grams - 1 tablespoon) in another cast-iron pan and when it becomes frothy, add the remaining salsify and juniper berries. Season with salt.

Zest the orange; set aside for garnish. Add the juice of the orange and 100 milliliters - 1/3 cup plus 1 tablespoon water, and cook for 10 minutes. Meanwhile, rinse, dry, and pluck the basil leaves; set aside for garnish.

Cook the scallops
Heat a little olive oil over high heat in a fry-pan and brown the scallops on one side for only 1 minute.

Finish and serve
Immediately transfer the scallops to 4 warmed plates. Arrange the salsify around them. Decorate with a few basil leaves and add grated orange zest. Serve immediately.

SALAD OF CUTTLEFISH WITH CRANBERRY BEANS

200 grams - 1 3/4 cups shelled cranberry (borlotti) beans
2 cuttlefish, about 500 grams - 1 pound 2 ounces, or squid
4 Welsh onions or scallions
2 sprigs thyme
2 sprigs rosemary
Salt
Freshly ground pepper
Olive oil
750 milliliters - 3 1/3 cups plus 4 tablespoons chicken broth (see p. 62)
2 sage leaves
2 cloves garlic
1 red onion
1 bunch flat-leaf parsley
2 pinches Espelette pepper
5 tablespoons sherry vinegar
1 organic, unwaxed lemon

AD - Cuttlefish requires very little cooking; otherwise they'll turn rubbery. If you can't find any, replace with squid, which also cooks very quickly.

PN - A fantastic, balanced, one-dish meal that I adore. It has everything. It's packed with carbohydrates with the beans, protein with the cuttlefish, very little fat, and loads of vitamins and minerals.

Prepare the beans a day ahead
Soak the beans in a bowl filled with cold water for 24 hours.

On the day the dish will be served, prepare the cuttlefish
Thoroughly rinse, dry, and finely slice the cuttlefish. Transfer to a dish. Remove the outer layer of skin from the Welsh onions. Cut off the tough green tops of the leaves and mince the rest. Spread them out over the cuttlefish. Pluck the thyme and rosemary and scatter over the cuttlefish. Season with salt and pepper. Add 4 tablespoons of olive oil. Mix well and marinate in the refrigerator for at least 30 minutes.

Cook the beans
Drain the beans and place in a saucepan. Add the broth, sage, and whole garlic cloves. Bring to a boil, lower the heat, and simmer for 30 minutes. Then season with salt and cook for 15 minutes more.

Prepare the onion and parsley
In the meantime, peel and mince the onion. Rinse, dry, pluck, and mince the parsley leaves. Set aside.

Finish and serve
Add the minced onion, Espelette pepper, vinegar, and grated lemon zest to the beans. Mix well. Transfer the beans to a serving bowl. Heat a little olive oil in a frying pan and quickly sauté the cuttlefish with the marinade for 1 minute while stirring constantly. Add the parsley and mix. Add the cooked cuttlefish to the bowl with the beans and mix gently. Serve from the bowl or on individual plates.

POT-AU-FEU BROTH WITH RICE PAPER DUMPLINGS

5 shallots
300 milliliters - 1 1/4 cups aged wine vinegar
350 grams - 12 ounces leftover meat from pot-au-feu (see p. 150)
300 grams - 10 1/2 ounces leftover vegetables from pot-au-feu (see p. 150)
1/4 bunch cilantro
Salt
Freshly ground pepper
1 teaspoon store-bought horseradish
8 rice-paper wrappers
1 carrot
1 turnip
1 liter - 4 1/4 cups pot-au-feu broth (see p. 150)
Olive oil

AD - You can use other kinds of leftover meat other than from pot-au-feu; it's a practical way to use up leftovers. The carrot and turnip strips add a very pleasant crunch and freshness.

PN - This recipe will delight those who are gluten-free because the rice-paper wrappers don't contain any gluten. Rice-paper wrappers can be found at Asian grocery stores and also in the international aisle of supermarkets and online.

Make the pickled shallots
Peel and mince the shallots. Put them in a saucepan, add the vinegar, and simmer until all the vinegar has evaporated and the shallots are well stewed, about 20 minutes. Cool slightly.

Prepare the filling
Shred the meat into a bowl. Chop the leftover vegetables into small pieces and add them to the bowl.

Rinse, dry, and pluck the cilantro leaves. Set aside about twenty leaves for garnish and mince the rest. Add to the bowl. Season with salt and pepper, and mix well. Then gradually add the pickled shallots. Taste the mixture as you add them and stop when the flavor is to your liking. Incorporate the horseradish. Taste the mixture again and adjust the amount. Mix.

Form the dumplings
Grease a large plate or tray with oil. Prepare a bowl of cold water. Soak each sheet of rice paper for 2 minutes to soften. Drain the sheet and place it on a cutting board. Cut it in half. Put 1 tablespoon (about 40 grams - 1 1/2 ounces) of filling on each half-sheet and fold over the ends to make a parcel. Transfer to the tray. Do the same for the other 7 rice paper sheets.

Finish and serve
Wash and peel the carrot and turnip and cut into small strips. Put the broth in a saucepan and bring to a boil. Heat 2 tablespoons olive oil in a frying pan over high heat. When the pan is very hot, add the dumplings and brown lightly on each side, then divide among 4 bowls. Add the reserved cilantro leaves and carrot and turnip strips. Pour some of the very hot broth over the dumplings and serve immediately.

SPINACH, WALNUT, AND RICOTTA LASAGNA

500 grams - 1 pound 2 ounces spinach
Salt
Olive oil
250 grams - 9 ounces/2 cups flour
1 egg
Freshly ground pepper
30 grams - 1 ounce/2 tablespoons butter
30 grams - 1 ounce/2 tablespoons flour
30 grams - 1 ounce/1/4 cup hazelnuts
200 milliliters - 3/4 cup plus 1 tablespoon lait ribot or buttermilk
15 walnut halves
150 grams - 5 1/2 ounces/2/3 cup ricotta cheese
2 tablespoons grated Parmesan cheese

AD - You can make the lasagna in advance and store them in the refrigerator. In that case, add 5 minutes to the lasagna cook time.

PN - Lait ribot is the liquid left after churning butter and it ferments naturally. It comes from Brittany.

Make the lasagna dough

Remove the stalks from the spinach and wash the leaves. Set aside 300 grams - 10 1/2 ounces of spinach leaves. Bring a large saucepan of salted water to a boil and prepare a bowl with water and ice. Immerse the remaining spinach (200 grams - 7 ounces) in the boiling water for 2 minutes, shock in the ice water, and squeeze with your hands. Place the spinach in a blender, add a little olive oil, and blend to a smooth puree. Combine the flour, egg, spinach puree, 2 tablespoons olive oil, and a pinch of salt in a large bowl. Mix with your fingers, then work the dough until it becomes smooth. Roll into a ball, cover with plastic wrap (cling film), and refrigerate for at least 3 hours.

Prepare the lasagna sheets

Roll the dough out to a thickness of 2 millimeters - 1/16 inch. Choose a baking dish measuring 25 x 18 cm - 10 x 7 inches and cut the pasta into rectangles of this size. Bring a large saucepan of salted water to a boil. Prepare a large bowl of water with ice cubes and a tray lined with a cloth. Immerse the pasta sheets, two at a time, in the boiling water, then refresh in the ice water. Spread them out over the cloth to dry.

Prepare the spinach

Heat a little olive oil in a sauté pan and add the reserved spinach leaves. Season with salt and pepper, and sauté quickly while stirring constantly.

Make the béchamel sauce

Melt the butter in a saucepan. Add the 30 grams – 2 tablespoons flour and brown it while whisking, then add the lait ribot. Whisk and cook for 2–3 minutes.

Assemble the lasagna

Preheat the oven to 190°C - 375°F (gas mark 5). Brush the inside of the baking dish with oil. Chop the walnuts. Lay a lasagna sheet at the bottom of the dish, cover lightly with béchamel sauce. Use a teaspoon to make successive layers of ricotta, sautéed spinach, and chopped walnuts. Lay another sheet on top and repeat the process. Top with an extra layer of béchamel sauce and sprinkle with the Parmesan.

Finish and serve

Bake for 30–40 minutes. Serve immediately.

ONION PANZEROTTI

500 grams - 1 pound 2 ounces/3 2/3 cups pastry flour, plus more for dusting
2 teaspoons baking powder
Salt
Olive oil
50 grams - 2 ounces/1/3 cup raisins
1 kilogram - 2 pounds 4 ounces red onions
1 stalk celery
2 bay leaves
4 anchovy fillets in oil
50 grams - 2 ounces/1/3 cup salt-packed capers
200 grams - 7 ounces/2 cups pitted green olives
6 pieces tomato confit (see p. 363)
Espelette pepper

AD - Panzerotti originated in Southern Italy. They're traditionally deep-fried, but this is our healthy version.

PN - They can be filled in many ways. But I love this filling made with onion, given the exceptional nutritional properties this vegetable has.

Make the dough
Mix the flour with the baking powder in a bowl. Gradually add 300 milliliters - 1 1/4 cups lukewarm water, 2 pinches salt, and 2 tablespoons olive oil while mixing constantly. When the dough is smooth, shape it into a ball and work it with your hands for 1–2 minutes, then roll it into a ball again. Transfer to a bowl and dust lightly with flour. Cover with a damp kitchen towel and proof for about 1 hour.

Prepare the ingredients for the filling
Soak the raisins in a bowl filled with hot water. Peel the onions and slice into rounds. Wash, dry, and remove the tough strings from the celery stalk, then cut the celery into small pieces.

Mash the anchovies with a fork. Rinse the capers, then chop them with the olives and tomato confit pieces.

Make the filling
Heat a little olive oil in a cast-iron pan. Sweat the onions and celery without browning for 5–6 minutes while stirring constantly. Add the anchovies and capers, olives, soaked raisins, and tomato confit mixture. Stir and cook over low heat for 2 minutes. Sprinkle with Espelette pepper.

Prepare the panzerotti
Knead the dough for 1 minute, just to stretch and fold, and then separate into two pieces. Roll the dough out to a thickness of 3 millimeters - 1/8 inch. Use a 10-centimeter- - 4-inch-diameter cookie cutter to cut out 6 disks. Transfer to a baking sheet lined with parchment (baking) paper. Cover with a kitchen towel and proof again for 30 minutes. Preheat the oven to 200°C - 400°F (gas mark 6). Spread 1/6 of the filling over half of one disk, then use a pastry brush dipped in water to moisten the uncovered dough. Fold the dough over and use your fingers to seal the edges, creating a turnover (panzerotti). Brush the top of the panzerotti with olive oil and place on a baking sheet. Repeat the process for the rest of the panzerotti. Bake for about 20 minutes.

Finish and serve
Transfer to a rack and let rest for 20 minutes. Serve warm or cold.

CREAMY POLENTA WITH OLIVES

SERVES 4
PREPARATION TIME: 10 MINUTES
COOK TIME: 45 MINUTES

500 milliliters - 2 cups
poule au pot (chicken) broth
(see p. 62)
500 milliliters - 2 cups
orange juice, preferably
freshly squeezed
200 grams - 7 ounces/1 1/2
cups polenta
Salt
Freshly ground pepper
1 organic, unwaxed blood
orange
1 sprig basil
50 milliliters - 3 1/2
tablespoons olive oil
3 tablespoons pitted black
olives
100 grams - 1 1/4 cups
grated Parmesan cheese

Prepare the polenta

Combine the chicken broth and orange juice in a saucepan and bring to a boil. Sprinkle in the polenta and whisk. Boil for 5 minutes while whisking constantly. Use a flexible spatula (scraper) to scrape any polenta sticking to the sides of the pan. Cover and turn the heat down to low.Cook very gently for 40 minutes, stirring from time to time. Add a little water if the polenta dries out too quickly. Season with salt and pepper.

Prepare the orange zest and basil

Wash and dry the orange. Use a vegetable peeler to peel off a fine layer of zest, taking care not to scrape off any of the pith. Chop the zest and set aside on a plate. Wash, dry, and pluck the basil leaves. Set aside the smallest leaves.

Finish the polenta

When the polenta is cooked, let it rest for 5 minutes, then gradually add the olive oil and stir well without causing it to reheat. Stir in the olives, Parmesan, and orange zest.

Transfer the polenta to a serving dish and scatter with the basil leaves. Serve.

AD - Squeeze the necessary oranges to make 500 milliliters (2 cups) of juice; that will be less expensive for you and better than a store-bought juice, even if it's only pasteurized.

PN - This polenta is practically a one-dish meal. The Parmesan provides enough protein so you won't need meat or fish in this meal.

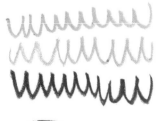

The two main varieties of celery we find nowadays, common or branch celery and celeriac, are descended from a single wild plant, smallage or wild celery, also known as marsh parsley, which has always grown in the swampy areas around the Mediterranean Sea. Over the centuries it was greatly used for its aromatic and medicinal properties, and also as an aphrodisiac.

Botanists in the 16th century had the idea of growing smallage covered in a mound of soil to blanch it and enhance its flavor, which is how common celery, which is also grown for its seeds, came to be. Celeriac appeared later, after efforts to enlarge its root. Both stalk and root vegetable have a potent smell and strong flavor.

● VARIETIES AND SEASONS

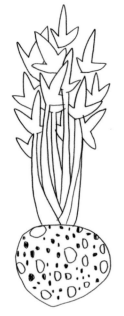

Common celery : Its well-developed and fleshy stalks are joined at the base to form a "head;" the plant grows to a height of 30-40 centimeters - 12-16 inches. The tender innermost stalks form the "heart." A subvariety is leaf celery, which is smaller. Celery is found year-round, but it is in season between the end of June and November.

Celeriac : Diamant, Giant Prague, and Brilliant are the more common varieties of celeriac in the United States, which appear in markets from early fall throughout the winter.

● CHOOSING AND STORAGE

The stalks of a head of celery should be firm and brittle, its leaves pale yellow and free of blemishes. A good celeriac is heavy and very firm. A spongy celeriac is old. Celery and celeriac can be stored in the refrigerator for a few days, carefully wrapped so that their smell does not taint other food.

● NUTRITION

Both celery and celeriac are low in calories, while containing a lot of dietary fiber, which makes them filling. Their legendary reputation as an aphrodisiac has yet to be scientifically proven.

● USES AND COMBINATIONS

Celery is both a vegetable (eaten raw or cooked), a condiment, and an aromatic. Celeriac has to make do with being a vegetable, used for soups and purees, and it can be eaten raw combined with a remoulade.

CELERIAC CAKE

SERVES 4
PREPARATION TIME: 15 MINUTES
COOK TIME: 1 HOUR

1 large celeriac
Olive oil
Celery salt
Freshly ground pepper
1/2 bunch chives

Prepare the celeriac

Preheat the oven to 170°C - 340°F (gas mark 3-4). Quarter and peel the celeriac. Wash and dry the pieces. Use a mandoline with safety guard to cut each piece into 2-millimeter- - 1/16-inch-thick slices.

Make the cake

Grease a 20-centimeter- - 8-inch-diameter round ovenproof dish with oil. Spread the celeriac slices over the dish and season every second slice with celery salt and pepper, and brush the slices with olive oil. Press down on each layer before starting a new one.

Bake the cake

Cook in the oven for at least 1 hour. Check that the celeriac is cooked through with the tip of a knife. It should slide in easily if the celeriac is tender. In the meantime, mince the chives.

Serve

Let the cake cool slightly, then sprinkle with the minced chives. Serve the celeriac cake in the dish or cut it into pieces. Accompany with an herb salad.

AD - Celeriac is a little difficult to peel. Cutting it into quarters makes the task easier. Keep your hand very flat (using the safety guard is preferable) when operating the mandoline so that you don't cut yourself.

PN - Celeriac is a legendary aphrodisiac, hence the old proverb: "If women knew the power of celery on men, they would plant it from Paris to Rome."

VEGETABLES COOKED IN SALT

SERVES 4
PREPARATION TIME: 5 MINUTES
COOK TIME: 1 HOUR

8 small leeks
4 carrots
4 artichokes
4 small yellow beets
(beetroots)
4 white onions
1.5 kilograms - 3 pounds 5
ounces/6 2/3 cups coarse salt

Prepare the vegetables
Carefully clean all the vegetables under running water,
removing all traces of dirt. Fill a bowl with water. Make
a cut along the green part of the leeks and shake them
in the water to remove any residual soil. Trim the top
of the leeks if they are tough. Do not peel any of the
vegetables, but dry them well.

Bake the vegetables
Preheat the oven to 190°C - 375°F (gas mark 5). Put
half of the coarse salt in a cast-iron pan with lid. Put
all the vegetables in the pan and cover with the rest
of the salt. Cover the pan with the lid and cook in the
oven for 1 hour. Check that each vegetable is cooked
through with the tip of a knife, and take them out as
they become crisp-tender. The vegetables should not
be mushy.

Finish and serve
As you take each vegetable out of the pan, peel and
transfer to a dish and keep warm.

Serve the vegetables warm with a condiment of your
choice, or with an herb vinaigrette.

AD – The vegetables shouldn't be peeled before cooking to
prevent them from absorbing too much salt. There's nothing
easier than making this dish. You can use any winter
vegetable with a thick skin.

PN – Here are simply cooked vegetables with all their
natural goodness. By accompanying them with an herb
vinaigrette and lemon juice, you'll enhance their vitamin
C. So good.

ADZUKI BEAN GRATIN

150 grams - 5 1/2 ounces/3/4 cup
adzuki beans
2 sprigs thyme
1 bay leaf
Salt
1 clove garlic
2 (5-millimeter- - 1/4-inch-thick)
slices pancetta
1 bunch scallions (spring onions)
Olive oil
2 tablespoons Dijon mustard
Freshly ground pepper
5 tablespoons bread crumbs made from
French country bread

AD - Adzuki beans are also known as Japanese red beans. They're popular in Asia because of their sweet flavor. If you can't find this type, you can make this dish with other dried beans, such as cranberry beans, flageolet beans, and so on.

PN - Like all beans, the adzukis are rich in slow-release carbohydrate, dietary fiber, minerals, and B-group vitamins. Here's a dish with very little fat, which is the way I like it.

Prepare the beans a day ahead
Put the beans in a bowl and cover with plenty of water. Soak for 12 hours.

On the actual day the dish is being served, cook the beans
Drain the beans and put in a saucepan. Cover with plenty of cold water (1 1/2 times their height). Add 1 sprig thyme and the bay leaf. Don't add salt. Bring to a boil, then lower the heat and simmer until the beans are soft, 1 1/2–2 hours.

Lightly season with salt at the end of the cooking process.

Prepare the pancetta and scallions
In the meantime, cut the pancetta slices into about 3-centimeter - 1 1/4-inch lardons. Trim off the tough upper part of the scallion leaves. Peel and wash. Quarter the white bulbs and mince the green leaves, setting them aside separately.

Cook the beans
Preheat the oven to 200°C - 400°F (gas mark 6). Heat a very small amount of olive oil in a cast-iron pan. Add the pancetta lardons and the quartered scallion bulbs and stir. Pluck the leaves of the remaining sprig of thyme into the pan and sweat for 3 minutes while stirring.

Place a strainer over a bowl and drain the beans. Add the beans to the pan with the pancetta and scallions and mix. Add a ladle of the bean cooking liquid, mix, and cook for only 2 minutes. Remove the pan from the heat. Add the minced scallion greens and mustard. Mix and adjust the seasoning with salt and pepper.

Bake the gratin and serve
Transfer the contents of the pan to a gratin dish. Use a flexible spatula (scraper) to spread the beans out evenly. Sprinkle with bread crumbs and bake the gratin for 15 minutes, until browned. Serve immediately.

VEGETABLE AND WINTER FRUIT GRATIN

SERVES 4
PREPARATION TIME: 25 MINUTES
COOK TIME: 40 MINUTES

1 small white onion
4 large white mushrooms
1 slice pumpkin (winter squash)
1 new turnip
1 Boule D'or turnip
1/2 head broccoli
1 small Agria potato
3 carrots in different colors
1 Cox's Orange Pippin apple
Olive oil
2 cloves garlic
Freshly ground pepper
6 sprigs flat-leaf parsley
6 sprigs chervil
1 sprig tarragon
20 grams - 3/4 ounces grated Parmesan cheese
Fleur de sel

Prepare the vegetables

Peel and mince the onion. Clean the mushrooms, trim the stems, and cut into about a 5-millimeter- - 1/4-inch dice. Wash and peel the pumpkin, turnips, broccoli stem, potato, carrots, and apple. Use a mandoline with safety guard or a sharp knife to cut the vegetables and apple into about a 3-millimeter- - 1/8-inch-thick slices.

Cook the vegetables

Preheat the oven to 180°C - 350°F (gas mark 4). Heat a little olive oil in a sauté pan with lid and sweat the onion for 2 minutes. Add the mushrooms and 1 crushed garlic clove, mix, cover with a lid, and cook for 6 minutes. Remove the garlic, season with pepper, and set aside. Peel the second garlic clove and rub it over the bottom of a gratin dish. Spread out the mushroom-onion mix-ture in the bottom of the dish, then distribute the other vegetables and apple slices over it, overlapping them and alternating colors. Cover the dish with aluminum foil and bake in the oven for 25 minutes.

Finish and serve

While the gratin is baking, wash, dry, pluck, and mince the parsley, chervil, and tarragon leaves. Grate the Parmesan. After 25 minutes, uncover the gratin and sprinkle with an even covering of cheese. Return to the oven, uncovered, until the Parmesan has browned, Remove from the oven, season with a generous grinding of pepper, and sprinkle with the minced herbs. Serve immediately.

AD - If you can't find a Boule D'or turnip, use 2 small new turnips with greens. You can use the other half of the broccoli for a soup.

PN - This dish gives you your full five servings a day of fruit and vegetables, which is a good thing. It's quite a substantial dish, but if you don't finish it, the rest can be easily reheated or turned into a soup.

ROASTED WINTER VEGETABLES

SERVES 4
PREPARATION TIME: 20 MINUTES
COOK TIME: 40 MINUTES

4 carrots
4 turnips
4 potatoes
2 red onions
1 yellow beet (beetroot)
1 small celeriac
8 cloves garlic
5 tablespoons olive oil
Salt
2 sprigs thyme
1 sprig rosemary
1 bay leaf
2 tablespoons honey
5 tablespoons wine vinegar

Prepare the vegetables
Preheat the oven to 190°C - 375°F (gas mark 5). Peel and wash all of the vegetables. Halve the carrots, turnips, and potatoes. Quarter the onions. Slice the beet and celeriac. Crush the garlic cloves.

Cook the vegetables
Combine the vegetables in a deep earthenware bowl and drizzle with the olive oil. Season with salt, add the thyme, rosemary, and bay leaf, and toss together.

Spread out the vegetables in a roasting pan or on a baking sheet. Roast for 40 minutes. Check the vegetables and lower the heat if you see that they are turning golden too quickly. Toss gently from time to time. Check that they are tender using the tip of a knife.

Finish and serve
When the vegetables are cooked, add the honey and toss. Deglaze with the vinegar and scrape the dish with a flexible spatula (scraper) to recover all the caramelized juices. Remove the thyme, rosemary, and bay leaf, and serve in the dish.

AD - Adapt this dish to include the vegetables you can find at the market. Don't think twice about using your hands to mix the vegetables so that they're completely coated in olive oil before cooking.

PN - This is a very filling dish. To round it off, it only needs a soft-boiled egg or small slice of cold meat, a cheese or dairy product, and a piece of fruit, and you'll have a perfectly balanced meal.

SWEET POTATO SALAD WITH CANDIED LEMON ZEST

SERVES 4
PREPARATION TIME: 20 MINUTES
COOK TIME: 40-50 MINUTES

1 organic, unwaxed lemon
1 teaspoon honey
4 sweet potatoes
200 grams - 7 ounces/3/4 cup plus 2 tablespoons coarse salt
1 red onion
40 grams - 1 1/2 ounces/1/4 cup peanuts
1 bunch cilantro (coriander)
1/2 bunch Welsh onions or scallions
2 fresh chili peppers
1 tablespoon Dijon mustard
Salt
Freshly ground pepper
1 organic, unwaxed lime

AD - There are different varieties of sweet potato: These tubers can be more or less elongated and rounded, while their skin and flesh can vary between white and red, with yellow, orange, and purple colors also possible.

PN - The more color a sweet potato has, the higher its content in antioxidant carotenoids, which are very beneficial for the skin and arteries. They always have a slight sweetness that recalls the flavor of chestnuts.

Make the candied lemon zest

Use a vegetable peeler to remove the zest of the lemon, taking care not to remove any pith. Immerse the zest in boiling water for 2 minutes, then strain and refresh under cold running water. Chop the zest and put it in a small saucepan. Squeeze the lemon and add the juice to the zest along with the honey. Simmer over low heat for 20 minutes.

Prepare the sweet potatoes

Preheat the oven to 220°C - 425°F (gas mark 7). Wash the sweet potatoes under running water and dry them. Cover a baking sheet with coarse salt; put the sweet potatoes on top of the salt. Bake in the oven for 20-30 minutes. Check that they are tender using the tip of a knife. The cooking time will vary depending on the size of the sweet potatoes.

Prepare the other salad ingredients

Peel and slice the red onion. Coarsely chop the peanuts. Wash, dry, pluck, and mince the cilantro leaves. Trim off the tougher green parts of the Welsh onions, remove the outer layer of skin, and mince. Chop the chilies.

Finish and serve

Peel the sweet potatoes and cut them into large chunks. Transfer to a salad bowl, then add the onion rounds, peanuts, cilantro, Welsh onions, chilies, mustard, and candied lemon zest. Toss gently and season with salt and pepper. Serve the salad on plates and grate lime zest over the top.

BEET TARTARE

SERVES 4
PREPARATION TIME: 30 MINUTES
COOK TIME: 5 MINUTES
REST TIME: 15-20 MINUTES

2 red beets (beetroots)
4 tablespoons tosazu sauce
(dashi vinegar)
4 tablespoons olive oil
4 salt-cured anchovy fillets
1/2 red onion
1/2 clove garlic
4 sprigs flat-leaf parsley
5-centimeter- - 2-inch-length
horseradish root
Salt
Freshly ground pepper

Prepare the beets
Peel the raw beets and cut into a small dice. Heat water in a saucepan and place a strainer in the pan. When the water comes to a boil, put the diced beets in the strainer. Cover the pan and cook for 5 minutes. Transfer the beets to a bowl, then drizzle with the tosazu sauce and the olive oil. Toss and set aside.

Prepare the rest of the tartare ingredients
Soak the anchovy fillets in a bowl of water for 15–20 minutes to de-salt. Peel and mince the onion and garlic halves. Wash, dry, pluck, and mince the parsley leaves. Peel the horseradish. Drain the anchovies and mince.

Finish the tartare
Add the minced onion, garlic, parsley, and anchovies to the bowl with the beets. Check the taste, and season with salt, if necessary, and pepper. Grate a little horse-radish into the bowl and toss again. Serve the tartare in the bowl or on individual plates.

AD - Japanese tosazu sauce is a mixture of rice vinegar, dashi, kombu, and dried bonito flakes. It has a light and pleasant smoky flavor. It can be found at Japanese grocery stores and online.

PN - People often overlook the nutritional benefits of beets. They have few calories and contain dietary fiber, B-group vitamins, and powerful and protective antioxidants, especially betalains, which are quite rare in food. Eat beets!

LEMON CURD

4 organic, unwaxed lemons
80 grams - 2 7/8 ounces / 3
3/4 tablespoons lemon flower
honey
1 heaping tablespoon
cornstarch
3 eggs
3 tablespoons olive oil

Prepare the lemons

Wash the lemons. Use a vegetable peeler to remove the zest from 2 1/2 of the lemons, taking care to keep the zest strips thin and without any pith. Squeeze all 4 lemons and put the juice in a saucepan with the zest.

Make the lemon curd

Add the honey to the saucepan with the lemon zest and juice and heat gently. When the honey has melted, add the cornstarch while whisking to prevent lumps from forming. Break the eggs into a small bowl and beat. Whisk the eggs into the pan with the lemon and honey. Turn up the heat slightly and cook, whisking constantly, until the mixture thickens and becomes creamy.

Finish

Transfer the lemon curd to a bowl. Let cool, then refrigerate until it is time to serve.

Before serving, stir the lemon curd and then drizzle with the olive oil. Do not mix in the oil.

AD - This recipe can be adapted to suit any citrus fruit. You just have to take care to reduce the amount of honey you use with sweeter fruits, such as oranges.

PN - This lemon curd is a real killer. Especially if you use a nice and fruity olive oil, which doesn't take away from the lightness of the curd. Serve it with tapioca flour crêpes (see p. 108) or with crunchy cereal cookies (see p. 107).

MANDARIN AND MANGO COMPOTE

SERVES 4
PREPARATION TIME: 15 MINUTES
COOK TIME: 15 MINUTES

8 organic, unwaxed mandarins
2 mangoes
2 tablespoons honey

Make the mandarin juice
Halve and squeeze 2 mandarins. Set aside the juice in a glass.

Prepare the mandarins and mangoes
Peel and pit the mangoes, then dice their flesh as uniformly as possible. Transfer to a bowl. Grate the zest of the remaining 6 mandarins into the bowl. Mix. Peel the mandarins and separate the sections (segments), taking care to remove all of the pith. Add them to the bowl.

Cook the compote
Transfer the contents of the bowl to a saucepan. Add the mandarin juice and honey, and then simmer until the fruit becomes very soft, about 15 minutes, but do not allow it to turn into a pulp.

Finish
Remove the pan from the heat and transfer the compote to a bowl. Serve warm or cold.

AD - If you can't find mandarins you can use organic clementines, which are very fragrant and delicious.

PN - This compote is a natural health food that will get you in good shape. Mandarins (and clementines) are full of vitamin C, as is the mango, which is not only a good source of this vitamin, but is packed with antioxidant polyphenols and minerals.

CHOCOLATE AND GINGER COOKIES

MAKES ABOUT 30
PREPARATION TIME: 20 MINUTES
COOK TIME: 7 MINUTES

450 grams - 1 pound dark
chocolate (70 percent cocoa)
100 grams - 3 1/2 ounces/7
tablespoons butter
50 grams - 2 ounces ginger
150 grams - 5 1/2 ounces
/packed 2/3 cup brown sugar
1 egg
3 grams - 1 1/2 teaspoons
salt
185 grams - 6 1/2 ounces/1
1/2 cups type 45 flour
15 grams - 1/2 ounce/3
tablespoons cocoa
Fleur de sel

AD - It takes a bit of effort to shape the cookies with a cookie cutter, but they are really elegant that way. And the ginger gives them an unexpected boost.

PN - Ah... chocolate! It works magic everywhere because of all the compounds it contains. It perks you up and protects against cardiovascular diseases. There's no end to the protective properties that are being discovered. You should never go without it.

Prepare the chocolate
Preheat the oven to 170°C - 340°F (gas mark 3-4). Grate the chocolate and divide into three batches of 150 grams - 5 1/2 ounces.

Make the cookie dough
Dice the butter and let soften at room temperature. Peel and chop the ginger. Combine the softened butter, brown sugar, egg, ginger, and salt in a bowl or the bowl of a stand mixer fitted with the paddle attachment. Mix. Add the flour and cocoa. Mix again. Incorporate 150 grams - 5 1/2 ounces of the grated chocolate.

Prepare the melted chocolate
Put 150 grams - 5 1/2 ounces grated chocolate in a heatproof bowl. Place the bowl over a saucepan with boiling water and let the chocolate melt.

In the meantime, heat the 100 milliliters – 1/3 cup plus 1 tablespoon water in another saucepan. When the chocolate has melted, whisk the hot water into it.

Form and bake the cookies
Line a baking sheet with parchment (baking) paper. Use your hands to form small balls of dough, each weighing about 30 grams - 1 ounce. Arrange them on the baking sheet, approximately 5 centimeters - 2 inches apart. Bake for 4 minutes, then take the baking sheet out of the oven. Use a spatula (turner) to turn the cookies over. Next, use a 6-centimeter- - 2 1/2-inch-diameter cookie cutter to give each cookie a perfectly round shape, then sprinkle with the remaining grated chocolate. Return them to the oven for another 3 minutes.

Finish the cookies
Make 3 dots of melted chocolate on each cookie, then add 3 flakes of fleur de sel. Transfer the cookies to a wire rack, then serve them on a dish or store in an airtight container for up to 4 days.

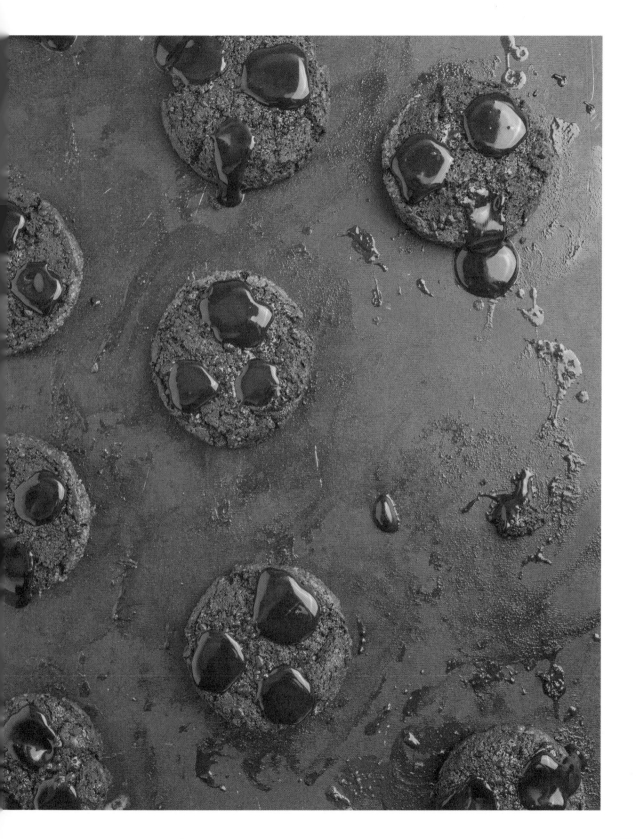

ORANGE PUDDINGS

SERVES 8
PREPARATION TIME: 30 MINUTES
COOK TIME: 55 MINUTES
REST TIME: 30 MINUTES

3 tablespoons golden raisins
(sultanas)
3 tablespoons dark raisins
50 milliliters - 3 1/2
tablespoons rum
200 grams - 7 ounces stale
bread
625 grams - 2 1/2 cups plus
1 tablespoon lowfat (2%) milk
400 grams - 1 3/4 cups crème
fraîche
3 tablespoons Grand Marnier
3 tablespoons orange
marmalade
1 vanilla bean
3 eggs
50 grams - 2 ounces/1/4 cup
superfine (caster) sugar
Butter
Flour

Prepare the raisins
Put the golden and dark raisins in a large bowl. Warm the rum and pour it over the raisins. Leave the raisins to soak up the rum for at least 30 minutes.

Prepare the bread
Preheat the oven to 180°C - 350°F (gas mark 4). Cut the bread into cubes. Put them on a baking sheet and toast until they are quite dark (but not burned), 15–20 minutes. Transfer to a bowl. Leave the oven on.

Make the puddings
Combine the milk, crème fraîche, and Grand Marnier in a bowl. Add the raisins and rum and the marmalade and mix. Split open the vanilla bean and scrape out the seeds into the bowl. Add the eggs and sugar, then mix to a smooth batter. Grease 8 8.5-centimeter- - 3 3/8-inch-diameter kugelhopf bundt cake molds with butter and flour and place on a baking sheet. Fill the bottom of the molds with toasted bread cubes and pour the batter over them. Bake for 35 minutes.

Finish
Take the puddings out of the oven and let cool. Unmold and arrange on a serving dish.

AD - Now that you have this recipe, you'll never again throw away stale bread. Any kind of bread is suitable for making these puddings: baguette, whole-wheat, etc. Serve these puddings with a fruit salad.

PN - If you're making these puddings for a child's afternoon snack (which would be far better than a pain au chocolat packed with fat), soak the raisins in water only, and don't add the Grand Marnier.

BLOOD ORANGE SORBET

SERVES 4
PREPARATION TIME: 15 MINUTES
COOK TIME: 1 MINUTE
CHILL TIME: 3 HOURS + CHURNING

4 organic, unwaxed blood
oranges
3 tablespoons honey
40 grams -1/2 cup plus 1
tablespoon powdered milk
3-centimeter- - 1 1/4-inch-
length ginger

Prepare the orange zest
Wash and dry the oranges. Put the honey in a saucepan and grate the zest of the oranges into it. Stir.

Make the sorbet mixture
Squeeze the oranges, collecting the juice and pulp, and remove any seeds. This should give you 210 milliliters - about 9/10 cup. Add the orange pulp to the saucepan. Add the 230 milliliters – 1 cup water and powdered milk. Peel and grate the ginger and add it to the pan. Stir and bring to a boil for 1 minute. Transfer the mixture to a bowl and refrigerate for at least 3 hours.

Finish the sorbet
Transfer the mixture to an ice cream maker and churn according to manufacturer's instructions. Store the sorbet in an airtight container in the freezer until it is time to serve.

AD - This sorbet can be made the same way with other citrus fruit. You only need to adjust the amount of honey, depending on the acidity of the fruit.

PN - I love it. The vitamin C from the oranges is kept intact. You can also pour the mixture into ice pop (lolly) molds and set them in the freezer. Very healthy for small (and big) kids.

Judging by the seeds found at many archeological sites, humans have been eating pears for thousands of years. They have existed since the Neolithic period and China began growing pear trees in about 4,000 BC. From the names given to certain varieties in the Middle Ages, such as caillou rosat ("pink stone") or poire d'angoisse ("anguish pear"), they were not really enjoyed . . . However, it is known that trees had been grafted and new varieties created since Roman times. But we would have to wait until the eighteenth century, and the talent of a Belgian monk, Nicolas Hardenpont, to finally have a juicy and tasty pear.

● VARIETIES AND SEASONS

There are several hundred varieties of pears in the world, only some of which are cultivated. The most common American pears include Anjou, Bartlett, Bosc, Seckel, and the very soft, very sweet Starkrimson. Varieties differ depending on the season, although the most common ones are eaten in winter.

● CHOOSING AND STORAGE

Pears are always harvested before ripening. This fruit is delicate and its flesh turns grainy if left to ripen on the tree. You should gently feel the fruit before buying: A ripe pear has soft flesh around its stem. But you also have to sniff them; their fragrance is more or less intense depending on the ripeness. Store them at room temperature.

● NUTRITION

Pears do not really stand out for their vitamin and mineral content. However, they are high in antioxidant flavonoids (unfortunately found in the skin which is often peeled and which is why buying organic is so important), dietary fiber (one pear has 2.3 grams - 1/16 ounce), and water. This is the reason for the French expression "une poire pour la soif" (literally, a "pear for your thirst," meaning to save something for a rainy day). A pear contains an average of 10 grams - 3/8 ounce carbohydrate per 100 grams - 3 1/2 ounces.

● USES AND COMBINATIONS

Once a pear is peeled and cut, it has to be rubbed with lemon to prevent oxidation. Pears go well with game and poultry, but they reign supreme in desserts, with syrup or wine, or in tarts. They are ideal with chocolate, especially the Bartlett or Bosc varieties. Pair with meat and poultry rather than fish.

PEAR CLAFOUTIS WITH PUMPKINSEEDS

SERVES 4
PREPARATION TIME: 20 MINUTES
COOK TIME: 35 MINUTES

3 eggs
50 grams - 2 ounces / 3 1/2 tablespoons pumpkinseed butter
60 grams - 2 1/8 ounces / packed 1/4 cup brown sugar
100 grams - 3 1/2 ounces / 2/3 cup rice flour
1 vanilla bean
250 milliliters - 1 cup coconut milk
250 milliliters - 1 cup soy milk
2 large pears

Make the clafoutis batter
Preheat the oven to 180°C - 350°F (gas mark 4). Break the eggs into a deep earthenware bowl and add the pumpkinseed butter. Beat, add the brown sugar and rice flour, and mix again. Split the vanilla bean and scrape out the seeds. Add the vanilla seeds to the bowl, then gradually whisk in the coconut and soy milks; whisk thoroughly. Pour the batter into four 8 centimeter- - 3 1/8-inch-diameter porcelain ramekins.

Prepare the pears
Peel the pears. Halve, core, and finely slice them. Arrange one quarter of the slices in each ramekin.

Bake the clafoutis
Put the ramekins in the oven and bake for 35 minutes. Serve warm or cold.

AD - Actually, this clafoutis can be made throughout the year with seasonal fruits—with raspberries in summer and rehydrated prunes in winter, for instance. And it's gluten-free.

PN - Pumpkin seed butter can be found at organic food stores and online. It's a gold mine of omega-3 and dietary fiber. It also contains a lot of minerals and B-group vitamins, along with the antioxidant vitamin E.

197

"NATURE" VACHERIN WITH CITRUS

SERVES 4-6
PREPARATION TIME: 40 MINUTES
COOK TIME: 8 MINUTES
REST TIME: 1 HOUR

About 200 grams - 1 cup blood orange sorbet (see p. 193)
About 200 grams - 1 cup lime sorbet (see p. 269)
1 egg, plus 1 egg white
40 grams - 1 1/2 ounces/3 1/2 tablespoons superfine (caster) sugar
1 handful sliced (flaked) almonds
1 organic, unwaxed lemon
2 organic, unwaxed pomelos
2 organic, unwaxed oranges
2 organic, unwaxed clementines
4 tablespoons olive oil
200 grams - 1 cup cream cheese
Espelette pepper

AD - This is the "Nature" interpretation of the vacherin by Christophe Saintagne. He shows full respect for the spirit of the dish, with crunch in the tuiles, softness in the cream cheese, and cold in the sorbets. And the result is lightness.

PN - I love it, naturally. Besides, it practically isn't sweet, but it's packed with vitamin C. The best of the best.

Make the sorbets
Make the blood orange sorbet (see p. 193) and the lime sorbet (see p. 269).

Make the almond tuiles
Mix the egg, egg white, and sugar together in a bowl. Rest at room temperature for 1 hour. Preheat the oven to 180°C - 350°F (gas mark 4). Spread an even layer of the mixture over a nonstick baking sheet and sprinkle with sliced almonds. Bake until golden, 6–8 minutes. Take the tuiles out of the oven and transfer to a wire rack.

Prepare the fruit
Grate the zest of 1 lemon, 1 pomelo, 1 orange, and 1 clementine into a bowl and set aside. Supreme and section (segment) all of the fruit over a bowl to collect the juice. Squeeze the fruit scraps with your hands to extract all the juice. Set the segments in a separate bowl.

Prepare the citrus vinaigrette.
Put the juice collected from the fruit sections in a saucepan. Place the pan over medium heat and reduce by half. Remove the pan from the heat and add the olive oil, while whisking briskly to make a thick emulsion. Keep warm.

Finish the vacherins
Arrange the fruit sections on individual chilled plates, then add 3 teaspoons of cream cheese over them.

Use two tablespoons to shape quenelles of blood orange and lime sorbet, and plate one of each in the center of the plates. Add a piece of the tuile and sprinkle with grated zest and a little Espelette pepper. Transfer the hot vinaigrette to a pitcher and serve at the table.

PRESERVED LEMON

MAKES 12
PREPARATION TIME: 30 MINUTES
REST TIME: 2 MONTHS

1.225 kilograms - 2 pounds 11 1/4 ounces / 6 cups plus 2 tablespoons superfine (caster) sugar
225 grams - 8 ounces / 3/4 cup salt
12 organic, unwaxed lemons

AD - Whenever possible, explore local varieties in your farmer's markets. Don't hesitate to buy them. Your preserved lemons will be even more fragrant.

PN - The preserved lemon rind is used to enhance stews, and the pulp can be used to season salads or crudités. It will allow you to use less oil. Preserved lemons are very good when creating light dishes.

Clean the jar

Bring water to a boil in a large cast-iron pot or a stock-pot. Put the jar and the lid in the pot and boil for 10 minutes. Put them upside down on a clean cloth and let it cool.

Make the syrup

Combine 2 liters - 8 1/2 cups water with 1 kilogram - 2 pounds 3 1/4 ounces / 5 cups sugar. Bring to a boil, then remove the pan from the heat and let the syrup cool.

Make the preserved lemons

Mix the salt with the rest of the sugar (225 grams - 8 ounces / 1 cup plus 2 tablespoons). Wash and dry the lemons. Starting from the top of a lemon, cut vertically into quarters, but keep the pieces attached at the base. Carefully spread them out. Place a large pinch of the salt-sugar mixture inside each one and close tightly. Stand the lemon inside the jar. Do the same with the remaining 11 lemons. Pack them tightly.

Finish

Add the rest of the salt-sugar mixture to the jar, then cover the lemons with sugar-water syrup. Place a weight (a glass full of water) on the lemons to stop them from floating and hermetically seal the jar. Store the jar in a cool, dark place for at least 2 months.

ARTICHOKES

ASPARAGUS

BEETROOT

CARROTS

CRANBERRY BEANS

CUCUMBERS

FAIRY RING
MUSHROOMS

FAVA BEANS

GARLIC

LEEKS

LETTUCE AND
OTHER SALADS

MORELS

ONIONS

PEAS

POTATOES

PURSLANE

RADISH

SCALLIONS

SORREL

TURNIPS

WELSH ONIONS

APPLE

RHUBARB

STRAWBERRIES

SP
RI
NG

TURNIP GREEN CONDIMENT

SERVES 4
PREPARATION TIME: 1 HOUR 15 MINUTES

1 tablespoon shallot
vinaigrette (see p. 116)
200 grams - 7 ounces turnip
greens (tops)
About 2-centimeter- -
3/4-inch-length fresh
horseradish root
Salt
Freshly ground pepper
100 milliliters - 1/3 cup
plus 1 tablespoon olive oil

Make the shallot vinaigrette (see p. 116)
Set aside in the refrigerator.

Prepare the dip
Carefully remove the stems and wash the turnip greens.
Coarsely chop the greens with a knife and transfer to
a blender.

Peel, wash, and grate the horseradish and add to the
blender along with the chilled vinaigrette. Season with
a pinch of salt and ten turns of the pepper mill. Blend
while gradually adding the olive oil, until the mixture is
smooth. Transfer the dip to a bowl, cover with plastic
wrap (cling film), and refrigerate.

AD - Tender and fresh turnip greens. Save them from
a bunch of new turnips and use them immediately. Adjust
the amount of horseradish to your liking.

PN - Turnip greens are full of vitamins, so it would be
really foolish to throw them away. Horseradish contains a
lot of vitamins and minerals. This dip is a real pick-me-up.

MINT CONDIMENT

SERVES 4
PREPARATION TIME: 35 MINUTES

2 tablespoons shallot
vinaigrette (see p. 116)
2 bunches mint
4 anchovy fillets in oil
1 tablespoon lemon juice
Salt
Freshly ground pepper
200 milliliters - 3/4 cup
plus 1 tablespoon olive oil

Make the shallot vinaigrette (see p. 116)
Set aside in the refrigerator.

Prepare the dip
Rinse, dry, and pluck the mint leaves. Put the leaves in a blender. Chop the anchovy fillets and add to the blender with the chilled vinaigrette, lemon juice, salt, and pepper. Blend while gradually adding the olive oil.

Transfer the dip to a bowl. Check and adjust the seasoning. Refrigerate until ready to use.

AD - Serve this condiment with small pieces of toast. It will also go wonderfully with boiled vegetables and poached or grilled fish.

PN - Mint is an almost magical plant with a great many properties. It's full of vitamins, antioxidants, and minerals. It can also relieve intestinal issues.

SORREL CONDIMENT

SERVES 4
PREPARATION TIME: 15 MINUTES
COOK TIME: 10 MINUTES

1 dash white wine vinegar
2 eggs
250 grams - 9 ounces sorrel
1 shallot
1 (30-grams - 1 ounce) cup
(pot) plain yogurt
7 tablespoons olive oil
Salt
Freshly ground pepper

Prepare the soft-boiled eggs
Bring water with a little added vinegar to a boil. Add the eggs and cook for 6 minutes.

Fill a bowl with cold water and ice cubes. Remove the eggs from the pan and cool in the ice water. Peel and transfer to a deep earthenware bowl. Mash well with a fork.

Prepare the sorrel and shallot
Wash, dry, and carefully pluck the sorrel leaves. Peel and mince the shallot.

Finish the dip
Add the sorrel, shallot, and yogurt to the mashed eggs and mix. Gradually add the olive oil while blending with a handheld immersion blender. Season with salt and pepper and a dash of vinegar. Transfer the dip to a bowl and refrigerate until it is time to serve.

AD - Use very fresh sorrel with no yellow leaves. The tartness of the herb is toned down by the sweetness of the eggs, but this condiment still needs to be sour. Be careful with the amount of vinegar you add.

PN - Sorrel rocks, nutritionally. It's packed with vitamins, minerals, carotenoids, and all kinds of other antioxidants. It's also high in oxalic acid, which makes it off limits to people with a tendency to develop kidney stones.

CUCUMBER SMOOTHIE

SERVES 4
PREPARATION TIME: 15 MINUTES

2 large cucumbers
5 sprigs mint
2 (150-gram - 5.3-ounce)
containers (pots) Greek
yogurt
Juice of 1 lemon
6 ice cubes
1 pinch Espelette pepper
1 pinch ground cumin

Prepare the smoothie glasses
Chill 4 large glasses in the freezer for 15 minutes.

Prepare the cucumbers
Peel and quarter the cucumbers. Use a teaspoon to scrape out the seeds. Then dice the cucumber pieces and transfer to a blender.

Make the smoothie
Rinse, dry, and pluck the mint leaves. Add the leaves to the blender with the yogurt, lemon juice, ice cubes, Espelette pepper, and cumin. Blend until the ice is completely crushed and the smoothie is perfectly smooth.

Finish and serve
Pour the smoothies into the chilled glasses and serve immediately.

AD - If you want to perk up this drink, add more Espelette pepper, and add a dash of vodka for a party drink. Serve this smoothie as an appetizer in place of a vegetable soup.

PN - Cucumber seeds can be particularly difficult to digest. But there's no need to remove them if you don't have this problem.

CRANBERRY BEAN SOUP WITH COCOA RAVIOLI

SERVES 4
PREPARATION TIME: 30 MINUTES
COOK TIME: 1 HOUR 10 MINUTES
CHILL TIME: 3 HOURS

400 grams - 2 cups cranberry (borlotti) beans
1 white onion
150 milliliters - 2/3 cup plus 1 tablespoon olive oil, plus more for pan
150 milliliters - 2/3 cup white wine
5 tablespoons white bread crumbs
1 tablespoon unsweetened cocoa powder, plus extra for serving
Salt
Pepper
Curry powder

Prepare the beans a day ahead
Put the beans in a bowl. Cover with water and soak overnight.

On the day the dish is being served, make the ravioli dough (see p. 366)

Make the bean soup
Peel and mince the onion. Heat a little olive oil in a saucepan set over high heat and sweat the onion without browning. Drain the beans and add to the saucepan. Mix, then add the white wine. Stir with a flexible spatula (scraper) to thoroughly deglaze the pan Cover with water.

Bring to a boil, then lower the heat, cover with a lid, and simmer until the beans are very soft, 40–45 minutes.

Make the ravioli filling and ravioli
Toast the dry bread crumbs in a frying pan until golden. Transfer to a bowl and add the cocoa powder. Mix. Add 3 tablespoons water and 1 tablespoon oil and mix. Use a teaspoon to make balls using all of the filling mixture and set aside in the refrigerator.

Roll out the dough into a long rectangle. Position the balls of filling in a line and spaced 5 centimeters - 2 inches apart on the top half of the dough. Fold the lower half over the top. Then use a 2-centimeter- - 3/4-inch-diameter cookie cutter to cut out the ravioli.

Finish the soup
Blend the beans with a handheld immersion blender while adding 150 milliliters - 2/3 cup olive oil until smooth. Season with salt and pepper. Keep hot.

Cook the ravioli
Bring salted water to a boil in a large saucepan. Immerse the ravioli in small batches and collect with a skimmer when they float to the surface.

Serve
Arrange the ravioli in bowls. Sprinkle with a pinch each of cocoa and curry powder. Pour the soup over and serve.

ASPARAGUS, SOFT-BOILED EGG, AND VINAIGRETTE

SERVES 4
PREPARATION TIME: 20 MINUTES
COOK TIME: 10 MINUTES

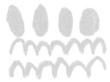

6 tablespoons shallot vinaigrette (see p. 116)
2 bunches green asparagus
Salt
4 eggs
1 bunch tarragon
Espelette pepper

Make the shallot vinaigrette (see p. 116)
Set aside.

Prepare the asparagus and soft-boiled eggs
Remove the scales from the asparagus spears. Cut off the tough end of the stem and peel to 3 centimeters - 1 1/4 inches from the tip. Set aside 2 asparagus spears. Tie the others into small bunches with kitchen twine. Bring salted water to a boil in a large saucepan and immerse the bunches of asparagus for about 6 minutes. Check that they are cooked with the tip of a knife, which should slide in easily. At the same time, boil the eggs in the same pan, also for 6 minutes.

Drain the asparagus on a clean cloth and untie. Take the eggs out of the pan and transfer to a bowl filled with cold water. When they have cooled somewhat, peel them.

Season the vinaigrette
Rinse, dry, pluck, and mince the tarragon leaves. Season the shallot vinaigrette with salt and Espelette pepper. Mix, then add the minced tarragon. Stir.

Finish and serve
Arrange the asparagus on four heated plates. Add 1 soft-boiled egg to each plate and make a small cut on the yolk with a knife. Drizzle with vinaigrette. Use a mandoline with safety guard to finely slice the reserved asparagus spears over the plates and season with Espelette pepper.

AD - Be sure to use asparagus grown as locally as possible. And take the time to heat your plates for 10 minutes in an oven set at 110°C - 225°F (gas mark 1/4). It's a worthwhile step.

PN - A nice one-dish meal, chef. The protein from the eggs is the best there is; asparagus contains a lot of vitamins, minerals, antioxidants, and dietary fiber, and so do the tarragon and shallots.

SPRING VEGETABLE CLAFOUTIS

SERVES 4
PREPARATION TIME: 30 MINUTES
COOK TIME: 1 HOUR 15 MINUTES

1 medium zucchini
1 medium eggplant
4 spears green asparagus
1 yellow bell pepper
1 red onion
300 grams - 10 1/2 ounces young peas, unshelled
Salt
Olive oil
3 eggs
55 grams - 1/3 cup plus 1 tablespoon flour
400 grams - 1 3/4 cups thick crème fraîche
160 grams - 5 2/3 ounces/1 2/3 cup almond meal (ground almonds)
1 sprig basil
1 sprig mint
1 sprig cilantro

AD – There's nothing to stop you from making this kind of clafoutis with other vegetables in winter. But this particular one can only be made with the last of the asparagus and the first of the peppers and eggplants. So make the most of them.

PN – A vegetable clafoutis is a really good idea, chef. It's a one-dish meal that I like a lot. And this one ensures that you get your quota of vegetables.

Prepare the vegetables
Cut the zucchini and eggplant into a small dice. Trim off the ends of the asparagus spears. Wash the spears and cut into 1-centimeter- - 1/2-inch-thick rounds. Use a vegetable peeler to peel the pepper, then cut the flesh into small pieces. Peel and mince the onion. Shell the peas.

Cook the vegetables
Bring a large saucepan of salted water to a boil and immerse the peas for 3–4 minutes and shock them immediately in ice water. Drain and set aside in a deep earthenware bowl.
Heat a little olive oil in a small frying pan and brown the zucchini. Add to the bowl with the peas. Put a little more oil in the frying pan and cook in the same way and in the following order the eggplant, asparagus, pepper, and onion.

Make the clafoutis batter
Preheat the oven to 180°C - 350°F (gas mark 4). Break the eggs into a bowl. Beat lightly with a fork, then add the flour, crème fraîche, and half of the almond meal (80 grams - 2 7/8 ounces / 3/4 cup plus 2 tablespoons). Mix. Pluck the basil, mint, and cilantro, and use scissors to coarsely cut the leaves. Add to the bowl with the vegetables and mix.

Bake and serve the clafoutis
Spread the clafoutis batter over the base of a gratin dish and sprinkle with the remaining almond meal. Spread the vegetables evenly in the dish. Bake about 40 minutes. Serve immediately in the gratin dish.

BAKED POLLOCK WITH OLIVE, LEMON, TOMATO, AND BASIL

SERVES 4
PREPARATION TIME: 20 MINUTES
COOK TIME: 15 MINUTES

1 (600-gram - 1 pound
5-ounce) fillet line-caught
Atlantic pollock
4 tomatoes
3 or 4 organic, unwaxed
lemons
150 grams - 5 1/2 ounces/1
1/2 cups pitted green olives,
preferably Nice
5 tablespoons white wine
5 tablespoons olive oil
1/2 bunch basil
Salt
Freshly ground pepper

Prepare the fish
Use a pair of tweezers to remove the bones from the fillet, then cut it into four 150-gram - 5 1/2-ounce steaks.

Prepare the vegetables
Quarter the tomatoes and remove the seeds. Wash and dry 1 lemon and cut it into thin rounds. Carefully remove the seeds. Quarter each slice. Squeeze the remaining lemons to yield 5 tablespoons of juice, and set aside. Bring water to a boil in a saucepan, then immerse the olives for 2 minutes. Drain in a colander and refresh under running water.

Bake the fish
Preheat the oven to 160°C - 325°F (gas mark 3). Combine the white wine, olive oil, and lemon juice in a bowl. Mix well.

Lay the fish steaks in a dish and pour the contents of the bowl over them. Distribute the tomatoes, lemon slices, and olives around the dish. Bake for 10–12 minutes.

Finish and serve
While the fish is baking, wash, dry, and pluck the basil leaves. Take the dish out of the oven. Check that the fish is cooked using the tip of a knife and season with salt and pepper. Scatter basil leaves over the steaks and serve immediately in the dish.

AD - Don't add salt to the dish; the olives do that for you.

PN - Menton lemons would be great, needless to say, even if they aren't easy to find. I've included 2 or 3 of them for the juice, but this can vary depending on how big they are.

MOREL OMELET

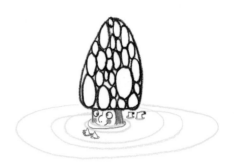

SERVES 4
PREPARATION TIME: 25 MINUTES
COOK TIME: 25 MINUTES

250 grams - 9 ounces fresh morels
250 grams - 9 ounces white mushrooms
10 grams - 3/8 ounces/2 teaspoons
butter
Salt
2 tablespoons vin jaune wine
1 red onion
50 grams - 2 ounces Comté cheese
8 eggs
500 milliliters - 2 cups milk
Freshly ground pepper
Olive oil

AD - Go easy with the salt. The mushrooms need very little because they absorb it very quickly. The Comté cheese will add saltiness later.

PN - Serve this omelet with a green salad that has chopped walnuts. It makes a very good combination. And it all makes a complete and balanced meal.

Prepare the mushrooms
Cut the stems off the morels and white mushrooms. Carefully wash the morels. To do this, soak them several times in a bowl filled with lukewarm water. Change the water until there is no more sand at the bottom of the basin. Drain in a strainer. Rinse the white mushrooms. Drain and quarter them.

Cook the mushrooms
Melt the butter in a sauté pan, then add the morels and white mushrooms. Season lightly with salt.

Add the wine, cover with a lid, and braise on a gentle simmer for 12 minutes. If the mushrooms dry out, add a few tablespoons water.

Prepare the eggs
Peel and mince the onion. Cut the cheese into a small dice.

Break the eggs into a deep earthenware bowl. Beat lightly and add the milk, onion, and cheese. Mix well, then add the cooked mushrooms. Mix again and season with a turn of the pepper mill.

Cook the omelet
Heat a little olive oil in a nonstick frying pan. Pour in the contents of the bowl and tilt the pan in all directions to spread it out well. While cooking the omelet, stir it and push the edges toward the center with a flexible spatula (scraper). Cook the omelet until it is done to your liking. Slide it onto a plate and serve.

PEA OMELET

SERVES 4
PREPARATION TIME: 15 MINUTES
COOK TIME: 20 MINUTES

100 grams - 3 1/2 ounces
young peas, unshelled
Salt
8 Welsh onions or scallions
1/4 bunch mint
8 eggs
20 grams - 3/4 ounces/1 1/2
tablespoons butter
Olive oil
Espelette pepper

Prepare the peas and onions
Shell the peas. Bring a saucepan of lightly salted water to a boil and prepare a bowl with water and ice cubes. Immerse the peas in the boiling water for 3 minutes. Remove and shock immediately in the ice water. Drain and set aside.

Peel the onions and trim off the tough part of the green tops. Finely slice.

Make the omelet
Rinse, dry, and pluck the mint leaves. Use scissors to coarsely cut them up. Break the eggs into a deep earthenware bowl, add the mint, and beat with a fork. Season lightly with salt.

Heat a splash of olive oil with the butter in a nonstick frying pan. Add the peas and brown over medium heat for 2 minutes. Add the onions and cook for 1 minute more. Transfer to a bowl.

Wash and dry your pan and place it over the heat with 1 tablespoon olive oil. Pour in the beaten eggs and tilt the pan in all directions to spread it out well. While cooking the omelet, stir it and push the edges toward the center with a flexible spatula (scraper). Cook the omelet until it is done to your liking. One minute before it has finished cooking, put the peas and onions in the middle. Roll the omelet onto a plate and serve.

AD - Keep the prettiest pea pods and onion leaves for a soup.

PN - That's good, chef. Everything used up, nothing wasted. That said, I really like this omelet that gives us a bit of everything for dinner. A vegetable soup beforehand, some dairy and fruit, and there you have a quick, well-balanced meal.

PURSLANE AND SHELLFISH SALAD

<u>SERVES 4</u>
<u>PREPARATION TIME: 30 MINUTES</u>
<u>COOK TIME: 2 MINUTES</u>

500 grams - 1 pound 2 ounces
purslane
1 liter - 1 quart (about
750 grams - 1 pound 10 1/2
ounces) mussels
1 liter - 1 quart (about
750 grams - 1 pound 10 1/2
ounces) cockles
4 large pink shrimp (prawns)
2 teaspoons mustard
Juice of 1/2 lemon
1 tablespoon wine vinegar
4 tablespoons olive oil
Salt
Freshly ground pepper
2 small onions

AD - Be careful when cooking mollusks. They should barely be opened, so that they keep all their lovely briny flavor. The more they are cooked, the more rubbery they become.

PN - Purslane is a small nutritional miracle because it's rich in iron, magnesium, vitamin C, antioxidant carotenoids, dietary fiber, and omega-3 fatty acids. You can't find all of that in any other salad leaf, except in mache.

Prepare the purslane
Wash and dry the purslane. Use a pair of scissors to detach the leaves, keeping the tender part of the stem. Set aside.

Prepare the shellfish
Wash and scrape the mussels. Rinse the cockles well. Put in a large saucepan over high heat and stir with a flexible spatula (scraper) to open them. As soon as the shells open, remove them from the saucepan and lay them flat on a tray or large dish (to stop the cooking process); let cool. Peel the shrimp.

Make the vinaigrette
Combine the mustard, lemon juice, and vinegar in a bowl. Mix, then add the olive oil. Season with salt and pepper, and mix well.

Finish and serve
Peel and mince the onions and put in a salad bowl. Remove the mussels and cockles from their shells. Add them to the bowl, together with the shrimp and purslane. Toss. Add the vinaigrette and toss again. Serve in the salad bowl or on individual plates.

GARLIC

Garlic is a perennial plant that has been grown and used for thousands of years. It produces a bulb, the head of garlic, comprising some ten to twelve cloves. Garlic can be stored for a long time.

● VARIETIES AND SEASONS

The most widespread species is **common garlic**, which can be white, pink, or purple. There are a great many varieties Aomori black garlic from Japan is pickled in sea water. **Green garlic** is the garlic shoot harvested at 3 months, before the bulb forms. **Wild garlic** is a wild plant that grows in woodlands and which is gathered in spring. The rarer **elephant garlic** has a bulb comprising between four and six cloves.

● CHOOSING AND STORAGE

A good head of garlic is always well rounded, with shiny cloves and without a germ growing out of it. Fresh garlic should be stored in the refrigerator. Dried garlic should be stored in a dry place at room temperature.

● NUTRITION

Extraordinarily nutritious, garlic has antimicrobial, antiallergenic, and antioxidant properties. It is beneficial for the cardiovascular system, delays aging of the cells, strengthens the immune system, and plays an important part in preventing certain cancers. A clove of garlic each day provides all of these benefits.

● USES AND COMBINATIONS

Use in marinades, for aromatic garnishes and sauces, with vegetables, in soups, with olive oil, to make pesto and aïoli, and for confit.

230

LEEK AND SKATE TERRIN

1 skate wing, about 500 grams - 1 pound 2 ounces
1 carrot
1 onion
3 stalks celery
3 leeks
1 clove garlic
1 bay leaf
1 sprig thyme
150 milliliters - 2/3 cup white wine
Coarse salt
Olive oil
Salt
Freshly ground pepper
150 milliliters - 2/3 cup Madeira
1 tablespoon capers
2 pinches Espelette pepper

Make the terrine a day before serving

Cook the vegetables and skate wing
Peel and carefully clean the carrot, onion, celery, and leeks. Set aside 2 whole leeks and coarsely chop the third. Coarsely chop the other vegetables .
Put 2 liters - 8 1/2 cups water into a cast-iron pot or Dutch oven. Add the carrot, onion, celery, chopped leek, garlic, bay leaf, thyme, white wine, and a handful of coarse salt. Bring to a boil, then simmer for 30 minutes. Rinse and dry the skate wing.
Remove the pot from the heat, add the skate, and cook for 10 minutes off the heat. Remove the skate and drain.

Prepare the leeks
Cut off the green leaves from the 2 whole leeks, then cut them lengthwise to make spaghetti-like strips.

Heat a little olive oil in a frying pan. Add the leeks and fry over high heat for 2–3 minutes. Season with salt and pepper. Add the Madeira and stir, scraping the pan. Set aside.

Prepare the ingredients for the terrine
Shred the skate flesh and put in a bowl. Rinse the capers and add them to the bowl, along with 2 tablespoons olive oil; mix. Season with salt, pepper, and the Espelette pepper. Mix. Retrieve the pieces of carrot and celery from the skate cooking liquid and cut into a small dice. Strain 100 milliliters - 1/3 cup plus 1 tablespoon of the cooking liquid.

Assemble the terrine
Make a layer of fried leeks in the bottom of a loaf pan. Scatter over some diced carrot and celery, then cover with a layer of skate. Alternate layers of fried leek, carrot and celery, and skate, finishing with the leek.
Press down with your fingers and shake the pan a few times. Add the strained skate cooking liquid. Tilt the pan to spread it out evenly. Cover with plastic wrap (cling film) and refrigerate for 12 hours.

Serve
When ready to serve, turn the terrine out onto a platter. Slice the terrine and serve on individual plates, or serve from the platter. If you prefer, you can serve directly from the loaf pan. Accompany with whole-wheat toast.

231

BULGUR AND ARTICHOKES

SERVES 4
PREPARATION TIME: 30 MINUTES
COOK TIME: 45 MINUTES

250 grams - 9 ounces/1 3/4 cups
coarse brown bulgur
Salt
6 purple artichokes
2 organic, unwaxed lemons
Olive oil
50 grams - 2 ounces/2 1/2 cups
arugula
2 sprigs mint
2 sprigs cilantro
2 tablespoons grated Parmesan
Espelette pepper
Freshly ground pepper

AD - The arugula adds quite a pleasant hint of bitterness. You can make this dish with white bulgur, in which case simply pour the boiling artichoke broth over it. There's no need to precook it.

PN - I prefer brown bulgur; it's richer in dietary fiber and minerals. It's worth the added effort of cooking it.

Wash, dry, and remove the stems from the arugula. Pluck the mint and cilantro leaves. Coarsely chop with a knife. Set aside.

Cook the bulgur

Add the bulgur to a saucepan with 250 milliliters - 1 cup boiling salted water, then lower the heat and cook for 10 minutes. Set aside in the pan.

Prepare the artichokes and make the artichoke broth

Turn the artichokes by paring the base to remove the largest leaves. Set the leaves aside. Cut the artichokes into six sections (segments) and remove the choke. Immerse one by one in a bowl of water with the juice of one of the lemons. Wash and dry the leaves. Heat a little olive oil in a saucepan and brown the leaves over high heat. Cover with water and cook for 10 minutes over high heat. Strain the broth into a bowl. Chop the herbs

Cook the artichokes

Heat a little olive oil in a sauté pan. Fry the artichokes for 5 minutes, turning over regularly. Season with salt and set aside.

Finish the bulgur

Pour the artichoke broth into the pan with the bulgur. Place the pan over medium heat and finish cooking the bulgur until soft, about 5 minutes. Remove the pan from the heat. Add 3 tablespoons olive oil and the Parmesan. Mix, then grate the zest of the other lemon over the top. Halve the lemon, squeeze the juice through a small strainer placed over the pan, and mix. Then add the fried artichokes, herbs, and arugula. Mix. Season with one or two pinches of Espelette pepper. Check and adjust the seasoning with salt and pepper. Transfer the bulgur to a large bowl and serve, or plate individually.

ORZO, SQUID, AND NEW VEGETABLES

SERVES 4
PREPARATION TIME: 20 MINUTES
COOK TIME: 25 MINUTES

5 scallions
8 very thin spears green asparagus
300 grams - 10 1/2 ounces young peas, unshelled
300 grams - 10 1/2 ounces baby fava (broad) beans, unshelled
1 handful snow peas
1 head broccoli
5 small squid
1 liter - 4 1/4 cups chicken broth (see p. 62)
Olive oil
Salt
350 grams - 12 ounces/1 2/3 cups orzo pasta
10 grams - 3/8 ounces/2 teaspoons butter
100 milliliters - 1/3 cup plus 1 tablespoon white wine
Freshly ground pepper
1/2 bunch flat-leaf parsley
1 clove garlic

AD - Orzo? This is the name given to pasta made from durum wheat semolina and given the shape of rice grains. It's also known as risoni, and puntalette in Italy. It's readily available at supermarkets, gourmet stores, and online.

PN - The perfect one-dish meal, with plant and animal protein; carbohydrate, vitamins, and minerals; and dietary fiber from vegetables, with little fat. What more can you ask for?

Prepare the vegetables

Cut the green scallion leaves 3 centimeters - 1 1/4 inches from the bulb (reserve the leaves for a soup), then peel the scallions. Trim the asparagus spears, keeping about 8 centimeters - 3 1/4 inches of tip. Wash them.

Shell the peas and baby fava beans. Remove the string from the snow peas. Remove 4 florets from the head of broccoli and wash them. Set all the vegetables aside.

Clean and cut the squid

Clean the squid (or have the fishmonger do it for you) and cut into about 1-centimeter - 1/2-inch slices. Set aside.

Prepare the orzo

Heat the broth in a saucepan. Heat a little olive oil in a cast-iron pot or Dutch oven and sauté the squid for 2 minutes over high heat. Lightly season with salt and transfer to a plate. Then put the scallions, asparagus, and broccoli in the pan and brown quickly. Add the orzo with the butter and mix well to melt. Add the white wine and cook until it is absorbed. Then add two ladles of chicken broth and cook, as if making risotto, until it is also absorbed. Continue to cook in this way for 5 minutes, then add the beans, peas, and snow peas. Cook for 10 minutes more, regularly adding broth. Check and adjust the seasoning with salt and pepper.

Finish and serve

While the orzo is cooking, wash, dry, and pluck the parsley leaves. Peel and mince the garlic clove. Mix with 5 tablespoons olive oil. Season with salt and pepper. Add this pesto to the orzo when it finishes cooking and mix well. Add the squid and mix again, gently. Serve the orzo immediately .

1 cucumber
1 avocado
12 tablespoons or 3/4 cup rice vinegar
9 tablespoons soy sauce
1 white onion
1 red beet (beetroot)
1 yellow beet (beetroot)
4 Tokyo Cross turnips
250 grams - 1 1/4 cups Japanese sushi rice
4 sheets nori
15 grams - 1/2 ounce/1 tablespoons wasabi
1/4 bunch chives
Pickled ginger, soy sauce, wasabi

AD - If you don't have a bamboo mat, use a sheet of plastic wrap (cling film). And don't put your sushi in the fridge; they'll dry out and lose their flavor.

PN - These nigiri and maki sushi will delight vegetarians. If you aren't one, serve them as an appetizer, and continue the meal with a cold meat and salad, a cheese, and a fruit.

VEGETARIAN NIGIRI AND MAKI SUSHI

Prepare the vegetables for the maki sushi
Peel the cucumber. Quarter it lengthwise and remove the seeds. Cut the flesh into about 2-centimeter - 3/4-inch-long batons . Transfer to a bowl. Halve the avocado and remove the seed. Peel each half and cut the flesh into small batons. Add to the bowl. Add 3 tablespoons of both rice vinegar and soy sauce to the bowl. Gently mix. Cover the bowl with plastic wrap (cling film) and refrigerate for 1 hour. Peel and finely slice the onion. Set aside separately.

Prepare the vegetables for the nigiri sushi
Peel and wash the beets and turnips. Use a mandoline with safety guard to slice them into 2-millimeter- - 1/16-inch-thick slices, then use a 3-centimeter- - 1 1/4-inch-diameter oval or round cookie cutter to shape them. Put the red beet slices on one plate, and put the yellow beet and turnip slices on another. Add 3 tablespoons of both rice vinegar and soy sauce to each plate and marinate for 20 minutes.

Cook the rice
Immerse the rice in a large bowl filled with cold water. Rest for 10 minutes, mix, and drain in a strainer. Repeat the process two or three times, until the water becomes clear.

Bring the 500 milliliters - 2 cups cold water to a boil in a saucepan and add the rice. Cook until all the water is absorbed.

Remove the pan from the heat and add 3 tablespoons rice vinegar. Mix gently to separate the grains of rice. Cover and rest for 15 minutes.

Make the maki sushi
Spread a sheet of nori flat on a bamboo mat and spread a little wasabi over it. Spread evenly with one quarter of the rice. Scatter one quarter of the onion over the rice, arrange one quarter of the vegetables down the middle.
Roll the mat carefully while holding the filling in place between your fingers until the edges of the nori sheet meet. Press lightly, then unroll the mat. Use the moistened blade of a knife to cut the roll in half, and then cut each half into three equal slices and arrange on a serving dish. Do the same with the other three nori sheets.

Make the nigiri sushi
Rinse and dry the chives. Take a small handful of rice and shape it into a sushi-sized ball. Place a slice of marinated vegetable on top, tie around the middle with a chive, and knot. Place the nigiri sushi on the serving dish. Continue in the same way until all of the rice is used up.

Serve
Serve both types of sushi accompanied by bowls of wasabi, pickled ginger, and soy sauce.

PASTA AND ARTICHOKE GRATIN

SERVES 4
PREPARATION TIME: 20 MINUTES
COOK TIME: 30 MINUTES

5 purple artichokes
Juice of 1 lemon
35 grams - 1 1/4 ounces/2 1/2 tablespoons butter
35 grams - 1 1/4 ounces/1/4 cup plus 1 teaspoon flour
500 milliliters - 2 cups *lait ribot* or buttermilk
Salt
Freshly ground pepper
300 grams - 10 1/2 ounces pasta (fusilli, penne, or rigatoni)
Olive oil
10 mint leaves
40 grams - 1 1/2 ounces/1/3 cup grated Gruyère cheese
40 grams - 1 1/2 ounces/1/2 cup grated Parmesan cheese

AD - Above all, don't forget about the pasta when you are boiling it; otherwise, you'll end up with a mush because it'll be overcooked. Set a timer or test the pasta often.

PN - There are twenty grams (3/4 ounce) of calcium-rich cheese per person in this dish. If you like, you can do away with a dairy product in this meal. A soup or vegetable appetizer to start, a soft-boiled egg or a slice of ham accompanying the dish, and a piece of fruit make a casual family dinner.

Prepare the artichokes
Remove the largest leaves from the artichokes. Quarter the artichokes, remove the chokes, and set aside, one at a time, in water with the lemon juice.

Make the béchamel sauce
Melt the butter in a saucepan, add the flour, and brown it while stirring Add the lait ribot and cook while stirring constantly with a whisk for 5 minutes. Season with salt and pepper and set aside.

Cook the pasta
Bring salted water to a boil in a large pot and immerse the pasta. When the pasta is just cooked (very al dente) drain and transfer to a bowl. Drizzle immediately with olive oil and stir well to prevent sticking.

Cook the artichokes
While the pasta is cooking, heat a little olive oil in a frying pan. Drain the artichokes and brown them on all sides. Season with salt and pepper. Wash, dry, pluck, and mince the mint leaves. Add to the pan with the artichokes and stir.

Make and serve the gratin
Preheat the oven to 180°C - 350°F (gas mark 4). Transfer the contents of the frying pan and the béchamel sauce to the bowl with the pasta. Gently mix, then transfer to an ovenproof dish. Mix the Gruyère with the Parmesan in a bowl and sprinkle this mixture over the gratin.

Place in the oven for 20 minutes. The The cheese should be melted and nicely browned. Serve in the dish.

CHARCOAL, ONION, AND ANCHOVY TART

SERVES 4
PREPARATION TIME: 1 HOUR 15 MINUTES
COOK TIME: 20 MINUTES
REST TIME: 1 HOUR

150 grams - 5 1/2 ounces
(1 1/4 sticks) butter
300 grams - 10 1/2 ounces/2
1/3 cups flour
1/2 teaspoon salt
1 teaspoon charcoal powder
10 salt-cured anchovy fillets
2 red onions
Olive oil
2 pinches dried oregano
150 grams - 5 1/2 ounces
arugula
Fleur de sel

AD - Charcoal powder turns the pastry black. It comes from burning saplings or coconuts at 700°C - 1,290°F without air.

PN - It's very commonly used (and has been for centuries) to alleviate bloating and different digestive ailments. Dough, onions, anchovies: that's a funny pissaladière you've got, chef.

Make the pastry
Take the butter out of the refrigerator, cut it into small pieces, and let soften. Put the flour in a bowl, add the salt and charcoal powder, and mix. Make a well in the center and put the butter inside it. Work the dough while gradually adding 80 milliliters - 1/3 cup warm water. Stop when all the ingredients are mixed and when the dough is consistent and roll into a ball. Cover with plastic wrap (cling film) and rest for at least 1 hour in the refrigerator.

Make the tart
Put the anchovy fillets in a bowl, cover with water, and soak for 30 minutes to remove the salt. Drain and dry with paper towels. Peel and cut the onion into very thin half-rounds. Put them in a bowl and season with a generous drizzle of olive oil and the oregano.

Preheat the oven to 180°C - 350°F (gas mark 4). Roll the dough out into a 30-centimeter- - 12-inch-diameter disk with a thickness of 2 millimeters - 1/16 inch. Transfer to a baking sheet lined with parchment (baking) paper. Arrange the anchovy fillets in the form of a rosette and fill in the spaces between them with the onions. Bake 15–20 minutes.

Finish and serve
While the tart is baking, wash, dry, and pluck the arugula leaves. Put them in a bowl and season with a drizzle of olive oil and a pinch of fleur de sel. Take the tart out of the oven and transfer to a platter. Cover with arugula and serve immediately.

WHITE ASPARAGUS AND CITRUS

SERVES 4
PREPARATION TIME: 20 MINUTES
COOK TIME: 15 MINUTES

2 bunches white asparagus
Salt
2 organic, unwaxed lemons
2 organic, unwaxed limes
2 organic, unwaxed pomelos
2 organic, unwaxed oranges
5 Welsh onions or scallions
5 tablespoons olive oil
4 pinches Espelette pepper

AD - Cut the asparagus spears to a length of about 15 centimeters - 6 inches; the rest of the stem is really too tough. The citrus and asparagus combination also works well with green asparagus. Taste the vinaigrette before adding the Espelette pepper and adjust the seasoning to your liking.

PN - The sourness of the pomelos and lemons is balanced by the sweetness of the asparagus and that of the olive oil. But if you're worried about it, replace one or two of them with an orange.

Prepare the asparagus
Trim off the hard ends of the asparagus. Peel and wash. Tie them into two or three bunches, leaving a long piece of loose twine. Meanwhile, bring salted water to a boil in a large saucepan. Immerse the bunches in the boiling water with the end of the twine tied to the saucepan handle. Cook for 5 minutes. In the meantime, fill a bowl with cold water and ice cubes.

Remove the bunches of asparagus from the pan and shock immediately in the ice water. Lay them on a clean cloth and untie.

Zest and supreme the fruit
Grate the zest of 1 lemon, 1 lime, 1 pomelo, and 1 orange over a plate.
Supreme and section (segment) all of the fruit, this time over a bowl to collect any juice. Also squeeze the fruit scraps to get all of the juice out of them.

Prepare the scallions
Trim off the root and tough part of the leaves from the scallions, and peel off the first layer of skin. Mince the scallions and set aside in a bowl.

Cook the asparagus and fruit
Preheat the oven to 180°C - 350°F (gas mark 4). Lay the asparagus side by side in an ovenproof dish. Fill in the space between each asparagus spear with the fruit sections. Pour two thirds of the citrus juice in a small saucepan and reduce slightly. Pour over the asparagus and put the asparagus in the oven for 6–7 minutes.

In the meantime, pour the remaining juice into the bowl with the onions and add the grated zest and the olive oil. Mix and season with salt and the Espelette pepper.

Finish and serve
Take the baking dish out of the oven and pour the scallion vinaigrette over it. Serve immediately.

BRAISED FAVA BEANS AND PEAS

<u>SERVES 4</u>
<u>PREPARATION TIME: 30 MINUTES</u>
<u>COOK TIME: 10 MINUTES</u>

1.2 kilograms - 2 pounds 10 ounces fava (broad) beans, unshelled
1.2 kilograms - 2 pounds 10 ounces young peas, unshelled
1 bunch small scallions
1 romaine (cos) lettuce heart
100 grams - 3 1/2 ounces smoked side (streaky) bacon
Olive oil
10 grams - 3/8 ounce/2 teaspoons butter
200 milliliters - 3/4 cup plus 1 tablespoon chicken broth (see p. 62)
Salt
Freshly ground pepper

Prepare the vegetables
Shell the beans and peas. Select the largest beans and set aside the smallest. Peel the scallions, keeping 5 centimeters - 2 inches of leaves, then wash and dry them. Separate the lettuce leaves and wash and dry them. Set aside the smallest, innermost leaves.

Make the dish
Cut the bacon into 2-centimeter- - 3/4-inch-square lardons. Add them to a cast-iron pot or Dutch oven with a little olive oil, and brown. Add the butter and melt, then add the scallions. Cook for 5 minutes without browning, turning them often.Add the peas, the largest beans, and the largest lettuce leaves. Stir.

Add the chicken broth. Cover the pan with a lid and cook over medium heat for 5–8 minutes, depending on the size of the peas. Taste the vegetables: They should all remain crunchy. Take the lid off the pan and reduce the cooking liquid until it is thick enough to coat the vegetables well. Check the flavor and adjust the seasoning with salt.

Add the smaller beans and lettuce leaves. Stir and remove the pan from the heat.

Finish and serve
Season the vegetables with a few turns of the pepper mill and stir. Serve in the pot or transfer to a large bowl.

AD - If you have time, peel the largest beans: Make a small slit on one side, then press between your thumb and index finger. The bean will pop out by itself.

PN - You can also sort out the smallest peas and set them aside with the small beans to add at the end. Get your children involved in shelling and sorting.

POTATO AND ONION CAKES

SERVES 4
PREPARATION TIME: 20 MINUTES
COOK TIME: 25 MINUTES

4 white onions
1 kilogram - 2 pounds 4 ounces fingerling potatoes, preferably Ratte
60 grams - 2 1/8 ounces / 4 tablespoons butter
Salt
Freshly ground pepper
Nutmeg
Olive oil

Prepare the onions and potatoes
Preheat the oven to 180°C - 350°F (gas mark 4). Wash, peel, and finely slice the onions. Set aside.

Peel and rinse the potatoes. Use a mandoline with safety guard to cut the potatoes into 1-millimeter - 1/32-inch slices and set them aside separately (without rinsing to preserve all of their starch).

Assemble the cakes
Melt butter in a small saucepan over low heat. Line a baking sheet (tray) with parchment (baking) paper.

Assemble the cakes: Make four ovals side by side, made of overlapped potato slices and measuring about 15 x 8 centimeters - 6 x 3 1/4 inches. Brush them with the melted butter.

Cover them with a layer of sliced onions. Grate nutmeg over them and season with salt and pepper.

AD - If you want to make a round cake, place a cake ring on the baking sheet and assemble the cake in the same way. The cake should be about 3 centimeters (1 1/4 inches) thick.

Cover with another layer of potatoes, brush with butter, add onions, season, and continue the same way until all of the vegetables are used up. Finish with a layer of potato slices.

Use small wooden skewers to hold the cakes in shape while cooking (the potatoes may slide off otherwise).

PN - Ratte potatoes are often twisted and not very easy to peel. Select the straightest ones; this should make life easier.

Bake and serve the cakes
Bake the cakes for 25 minutes, but check that they are cooked through using the tip of a knife. The potatoes should be very tender and the onions soft. Serve the cakes on a platter or on individual plates.

POTATOES

The potato is one of the most widely consumed vegetable in the world. It was grown in the Andes for thousands of years before being discovered by European explorers in the sixteenth century and taken back to Europe. But they were slow to become accepted because people feared that they caused insanity.

● VARIETIES
The great many varieties of potatoes come in different sizes, colors, and seasonal variations. They are usually grouped into two main categories: waxy or salad potatoes, and baking potatoes, whose starchy or floury flesh falls apart more easily.

● CHOOSING AND STORAGE
A good potato is quite firm, without sprouting eyes or traces of greening (solanine) which turns it bitter. This develops in light after the potatoes are washed, when they are no longer protected by the soil. This is why they should always be kept in a dark place.

● NUTRITION
Potatoes contain a lot of carbohydrates but are low in calories—they contain no natural fat. They provide some protein, minerals, and vitamins (including vitamin C). Potatoes are a food of choice for a balanced diet, except when deep-fried and saturated with fat.

● USES AND COMBINATIONS
Whether plain, with or without skin, mashed, gratinéed, sautéed, braised, or deep-fried, potatoes go with everything.

BEER-BRAISED YOUNG LEEKS

SERVES 4
PREPARATION TIME: 20 MINUTES
COOK TIME: 15 MINUTES

12 young leeks
20 grams - 3/4 ounces/1 1/2
tablespoons butter
Olive oil
1 clove garlic
120 milliliters - 1/2 cup
lager beer
4 thin slices walnut bread
1 slice smoked ham
1 teaspoon mustard
Salt
Freshly ground pepper

AD - This recipe can actually be made year-round. If your leeks aren't really young and are a little too large, cut off the top of the leaves, which will be too tough.

PN - Ah, leeks. The "stomach broom," as the saying goes but also the truth, because their fibers are beneficial for the digestive tract. That said, they're rich in antioxidants and vitamin C.

Prepare the leeks

Fill the sink with water. Cut off the base of the leeks and make a few incisions with a knife lengthwise in the leaves. Wash the leeks in the sink, shaking well.

Meanwhile, bring salted water to a boil in a saucepan. Immerse the clean leeks in the boiling water for 10 minutes. Prepare a bowl with water and ice cubes. Take the leeks out with a skimmer and immediately shock in the ice water. Drain well.

Cook the leeks

Heat the butter and a little olive oil in a cast-iron pan. Crush the garlic clove. Put the leeks in the pan, with the garlic clove, season with salt, and cook until lightly browned, about 5 minutes.

Add the beer, stir a little to deglaze the caramelized juices, then baste the leeks several times with a spoon to glaze. Transfer the leeks to a serving dish with a slotted spoon. Keep the leeks warm.

Finish and serve

Cut the ham into a small dice. Remove the garlic clove from the pan. Add the mustard to the cooking liquid and mix until well dissolved. Add the diced ham and stir for 1-2 minutes to heat.

Meanwhile, toast the slices of walnut bread, then cut into croutons.

Pour the sauce over the leeks. Scatter the croutons over the dish and serve immediately.

ROASTED ONIONS STUFFED WITH MINT

SERVES 4
PREPARATION TIME: 15 MINUTES
COOK TIME: 1 HOUR

16 salt-cured anchovy fillets
8 red onions
1/2 bunch fresh mint
Olive oil
Freshly ground pepper

Prepare the onions
Preheat the oven to 150°C - 300°F (gas mark 2). Rinse the anchovies in a bowl filled with water to remove the salt.

Peel the onions. Halve them vertically, but cutting only to the base, not through it. Cut each half in two in the same way so that the onions open like a flower. Place them in an ovenproof dish, base side down.

Rinse the anchovies well in running water. Wash, dry, and pluck the mint leaves and halve them. Alternate pieces of mint and anchovy fillets inside the onion flowers. Drizzle with olive oil.

Roast the onions
Put the dish in the oven for at least 1 hour. Baste several times. Check that the onions are cooked through. They are tender when a knife slides in easily.

Finish and serve
Take the dish out of the oven. Sprinkle generously with freshly ground pepper. Serve the onions in the dish or on individual plates.

AD - These onions are a good accompaniment for a Sunday roast chicken. Don't add salt; even when desalted, the anchovies will suffice.

PN - I love onion dishes. I've already explained that onions are a truly natural health food, so I won't say it again.

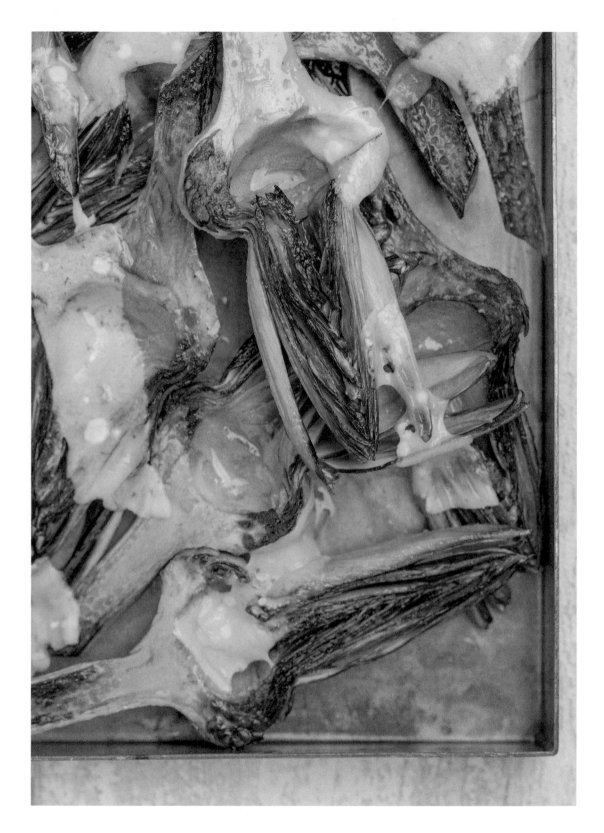

GRILLED POIVRADE ARTICHOKES

SERVES 4
PREPARATION TIME: 30 MINUTES
COOK TIME: 4 MINUTES

12 poivrade artichokes
1 lemon
Olive oil
Salt
40 grams - 1 1/2 ounces
Parmesan cheese

Prepare the artichokes
Turn the artichokes: Cut the stem 5 centimeters - 2 inches from their base. Discard the outer leaves. Use a paring knife to peel around the base. Cut off the remaining leaves from the top. Then halve each artichoke lengthwise. Remove the choke from the middle with a teaspoon.

After preparing each artichoke, rub with half a lemon to prevent them from turning black, and transfer to a dish. Brush olive oil over their entire surface, and then season with salt.

Cook and serve
Put the artickokes on a very hot flat-top grill, cut side down. Grill for 3 minutes, then turn and sear for 1 minute more.

Transfer the grilled artichokes to a dish and use a vegetable peeler to shave the Parmesan over the top. Serve immediately.

AD - The poivrade artichokes have to be super fresh. Otherwise they'll be too tough to grill this way. If you don't have a flat-top or other grill, cook them in a nonstick frying pan lightly brushed with olive oil.

PN - Here's a good vegetable to accompany a grilled or steamed fish, or a roast chicken. Simply brushed with olive oil, it's as light as it gets, extremely lowfat.

VEGETABLE SPAGHETTI WITH HEMP SEEDS

SERVES 4
PREPARATION TIME: 20 MINUTES
COOK TIME: 5 MINUTES

50 grams - 2 ounces/1/3 cup plus 1 tablespoon hemp seeds, chopped
1/2 celeriac
2 carrots
2 zucchini
1 organic, unwaxed lemon
1/2 bunch cilantro
1/2 bunch mint
Olive oil
Salt
2 pinches Espelette pepper

AD - Hemp seeds are produced by the hemp plant, which is related to cannabis, although it only contains 0.2 percent THC, the psychoactive molecule found in cannabis. Its growing is obviously highly regulated.

PN - There's nothing stopping you from getting a kick out of this dish. Hemp seeds contain a great deal of essential fatty acids, carotenoids, and vitamins. They're very good for you, just like sesame seeds.

Toast the hemp seeds
Preheat the oven to 160°C - 325°F (gas mark 3).

Put the hemp seeds on a baking sheet and put in the oven until they turn a light golden color, about 10 minutes.

Prepare the vegetables
Peel, wash, and dry the celeriac, carrots, and zucchini. Use a mandoline with safety guard to cut them lengthwise into 2-millimeter- - 1/16-inch-thick slices. Use a knife to cut the slices into long spaghetti-like strips. As they are cut, put the vegetable spaghetti in a bowl, and then toss.

Prepare the lemon and herbs
Finely grate the zest of the lemon and set aside on a plate. Squeeze the lemon. Rinse, dry, and pluck the cilantro and mint leaves.

Cook the vegetable spaghetti
Heat 3 tablespoons olive oil in a frying pan. Add all the vegetables at the same time, toss together, and sauté for 2–3 minutes. Season with salt and deglaze with the lemon juice. Add the herbs, grated zest, and Espelette pepper. Gently mix.

Finish and serve
Transfer the contents of the pan to a serving dish or arrange on individual plates. Sprinkle with the hemp seeds and serve immediately.

SPRING VEGETABLE TARTARE

SERVES 4
PREPARATION TIME: 30 MINUTES
COOK TIME: 2 MINUTES

300 grams - 10 1/2 ounces
baby fava (broad) beans,
unshelled
300 grams - 10 1/2 ounces
young peas, unshelled
1 bunch radish (approximately
300g - 10 1/2 ounces with
leaves)
1 bunch cilantro
4 new carrots
4 new turnips
1/2 bunch sorrel
2 new onions
4 tablespoons sorrel
condiment (see p. 209)
Salt
Pepper

Prepare the baby fava beans and peas
Shell and peel the beans. Set aside in a bowl. Shell the
peas. Bring salted water to a boil in a saucepan and
prepare a bowl with water and ice cubes.

Immerse the peas in the boiling water for 2 minutes,
then remove with a skimmer and shock in the ice water.
Drain and add to the bowl with the beans.

Prepare the other vegetables
Cut off the leaves, scrape, and wash the radish. Wash
and peel the carrots and turnips. Rinse, dry, and pluck
the sorrel leaves. Trim and wash the onions.
Finely dice the carrots, turnips, and onions and add to
the bowl with the peas and beans.

Finish the tartare
Add the sorrel condiment and mix everything well.
Season with salt and pepper. Serve very cold in the
bowl or serve the tartare on individual plates.

AD - If your baby fava beans are very small, then
there's no need to peel them. As usual with these vegetables, reserve the nicest and tenderest bean and pea
pods, together with the carrot greens (tops), for a soup.

PN - If you've had problems with kidney stones, you
should know that sorrel, which contains a lot of oxalic
acid, can contribute to their formation. Replace it with
baby spinach and a little basil pesto.

STRAWBERRIES

This fleshy little fruit has been subjected to every possible botanical travesty to satisfy the whims of the market. The forerunner to the strawberry that we know today is the wild strawberry, which once grew everywhere, including the greenhouses of the palace of Versailles for King Louis XIV. In 1713 the naval officer Amédée Frézier (aptly named given that Frézier is pronounced the same as strawberry plant in French) brought back plants from Chile that resembled strawberry plants that bore large white fruit. Planted in Brittany not far from Virginia strawberries (brought back one hundred years previously by Jacques Cartier), they were immediately pollinated by the others to produce a new variety with large red fruits, which were grown in Ploustagel and became the mother of the present-day strawberry. The strawberry was eaten locally until the mid-twentieth century. Dozens of varieties were subsequently developed, bearing downy and insipid fruits that were suited to large-scale production and shipping.

● CHOOSING AND STORAGE
Choose freshly picked strawberries that are shiny and with a bright green hull. The darker the fruit, the riper it is. Strawberries can keep reasonably well for a day or two in the refrigerator.

● NUTRITION
Strawberries are high in vitamin C, gentle dietary fiber (the pectin from their seeds), minerals, and antioxidants.

● USES AND COMBINATIONS
In pastries, or plain with sugar and/or cream, or with orange juice. Strawberries go very well with pepper, chocolate, and mint.

STRAWBERRY SALAD

SERVES 4
PREPARATION TIME: 15 MINUTES
REST TIME: 30 MINUTES

500 grams - 1 pound 2 ounces
strawberries, preferably
Gariguette or Mara de Bois
2 tablespoons honey
Juice of 1 lemon
4 tablespoons olive oil
2 sprigs small-leaf basil
5 cubeb berries

Prepare the strawberries
Wash and hull the strawberries. Halve the larger ones, and put all the strawberries in a salad bowl.

Make the dressing and pluck the basil
Combine the honey, lemon juice, and olive oil in a bowl. Beat well with a fork to mix. Wash, dry, and pluck the basil leaves.

Finish
Finely chop the cubeb berries, or put them in a pepper mill. Pour the dressing over the strawberries and mix gently. Scatter a few basil leaves over them, and add two pinches of cubeb. Mix gently and rest for 30 minutes before serving at room temperature.

Serve
Make a pretty arrangement with the strawberries on plates, or simply serve them in the bowl.

AD - Cubeb is also known as tailed or Java pepper. It comes from the island of Java. It has little heat, but it's quite bitter and very pungent. Use it sparingly.

PN - This dessert has vitamin C by the bucket load, because strawberries contain even more of it than citrus fruit. If you're diabetic (or a sugar phobe), reduce the amount of honey, or don't use it at all.

SUGAR-CRUSTED RHUBARB

SERVES 4
PREPARATION TIME: 15 MINUTES
COOKING TIME: 50 MINUTES

4 rhubarb stalks
800 grams - 1 pound 12
ounces/packed 3 2/3 cups
brown sugar
2 egg whites
1 (8-gram - 1/4-oz) envelope
(sachet) vanilla sugar
1 tablespoon honey

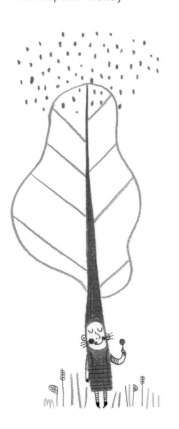

Prepare the rhubarb
Preheat the oven to 180°C - 350°F (gas mark 4). Peel and rinse the rhubarb.

Make the sugar crust
Put the brown sugar in a bowl, add the egg whites, and mix well.

Make the sugar-crusted rhubarb
Put half of the sugar crust mixture in a baking dish and spread it out evenly. Line up the rhubarb stalks over it. Sprinkle with the vanilla sugar, and use a teaspoon to make a line of honey on each stalk.

Cover with the rest of the sugar crust mixture, taking care that it forms a layer at least 1 centimeter - 1/3 inch thick over the entire surface of the dish. Bake for 45–50 minutes.

Finish and serve
Let the dish cool a little, then break the sugar crust to loosen the rhubarb stalks and serve in the dish.

AD - This rhubarb can be accompanied with cream cheese. And if you add a little grated ginger, it will be even more delicious. The two flavors marry quite well.

PN - Rhubarb was once used as a purgative-in high doses, of course. It is high in dietary fiber and is good for colon health.

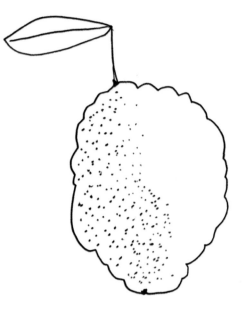

LIME SORBET

SERVES 4
PREPARATION TIME: 15 MINUTES
COOK TIME: 1 MINUTE
CHILL TIME: 3 HOURS + CHURNING

8 organic, unwaxed limes
4 tablespoons honey
300 milliliters - 1 1/4 cups water
40 grams - 1 1/2 ounces / 1/2 cup plus 1 tablespoon powdered milk
1 tablespoon cream cheese

Prepare the limes
Wash and dry the limes. Put the honey in a bowl and grate the zest of the limes into it. Mix. Squeeze all the limes over a measuring cup, collecting the pulp at the same time, and remove any seeds. This should give you 110 milliliters - about 1/2 cup.

Make the sorbet mixture
Put the lime pulp in a saucepan. Add the honey and grated lime zest, the water and powdered milk to the pan. Mix well and bring to a boil; boil for 1 minute. Transfer to a bowl and refrigerate for at least 3 hours.

Finish the sorbet
Use a handheld blender to mix the cream cheese into the sorbet mixture. Taste the mixture and adjust the sweetness with a little honey, if needed. Transfer the mixture to an ice cream maker and churn according to the manufacturer's instructions. Store the sorbet in an airtight container in the freezer until it is time to serve.

AD - This sorbet can also be made using lemons. In this case, add a little less honey because lemons aren't as sour as limes.

PN - This sorbet gives you a real shot of vitamin C. As people often feel fatigue in spring, this will work wonders. Serve it with a fruit salad (apple, pear, banana). It's a delicious flavor combination.

SORREL SORBET

SERVES 4-6
PREPARATION TIME: 15 MINUTES
COOK TIME: 5 MINUTES
+ CHURNING

500 grams - 1 pound 2 ounces sorrel
2 tablespoons superfine (caster) sugar
90 milliliters - 1/3 cup plus 2 teaspoons lemon juice
200 grams - 7 ounces/1 cup cream cheese (40 percent fat)
1 pinch salt

Prepare the sorrel
Wash, dry, and pluck the sorrel leaves.

Make the sorbet
In a saucepan, combine 110 milliliters - 1/2 cup water with the sugar and lemon juice. Stir and bring to a boil. Fill a large bowl with water and plenty of ice cubes, and place another bowl over it. Pour the contents of the pan into the top bowl and stir briskly with a whisk to cool quickly.

When cold, transfer the mixture to a blender. Add the cream cheese and sorrel. Blend until smooth.

Transfer the mixture to an ice cream maker and churn according to the manufacturer's instructions.

Serve
When the sorbet is made, serve it immediately in small ice cream bowls—this is when it is at its best.

AD - This very unusual sorbet has a flavor that is quite like that of green banana. You can imagine it accompanied with a chocolate sauce and crêpes (see p. 108).

PN - Wow! What a fantastic dessert. Did you know that sorrel is a gold mine of vitamins and antioxidants that are great for your skin? It's priceless. And besides, there's practically no sugar. It's great for anyone who is watching his or her waistline.

PICKLED WELSH ONIONS

MAKES ENOUGH TO FILL ONE 2-LITER - 67.6-FLUID-OUNCE JAR

PREPARATION TIME: 50 MINUTES

8 bunches Welsh onions or scallions

3 cloves garlic

1 teaspoon peppercorns

1 sprig savory

1.5 liters - 6 1/3 cups white wine vinegar

Clean the jar

Bring water to a boil in a large cast-iron pot or a stockpot. Put the jar and the lid in the pot and boil for 10 minutes. Put them upside down on a clean cloth and let it cool.

Prepare the onions

To peel the onions, cut off the roots and remove the outer layer of skin. Trim off about 10 centimeters - 4 inches of leaves, which will be too tough. Peel the garlic cloves and remove the green core.

Pack the onions tightly in the sterilized jar. Add the garlic cloves and the sprig of savory.

Pickle the onions

Bring the vinegar to a simmer in a saucepan. Pour it over the onions. Pour the peppercorns in the jar. Close the jar and turn it upside down on a clean cloth. Leave the jar untouched until the vinegar is cold. Then turn the jar upright and store it in a cupboard for at least 1 month before use.

AD - The Welsh onion is called a cébette in the south of France. It's from the same family as the chive. Its scientific name is Alium fistulosum, and it's also known as "bunching onion" and "ciboule onion."

PN - The Welsh onion has a very elongated bulb, which clearly distinguishes it from the small scallion, which is also sold in bunches like Welsh onions. But they're all from the allium family, one of the characteristics of which is their high antioxidant content.

ARTICHOKES IN OIL

MAKES ENOUGH TO FILL ONE 2-LITER - 67.6-FLUID-OUNCE JAR
PREPARATION TIME: 40 MINUTES
COOK TIME: 1 HOUR

25 poivrade artichokes
Juice of 2 lemons
500 milliliters - 2 cups white wine
1 head garlic
5 bay leaves
5 black peppercorns
5 juniper berries
1.5 liters - 6 1/3 cups olive oil

Sterilize the jar
Put the jar in a large cast-iron pot or a stockpot with the lid and cover with water. Cover the pot and bring the water to a boil. Then keep at a boil for 1 hour. Let the jar cool in the water, then store in a cupboard.

Prepare the artichokes
Remove the outer leaves, then cut the stem to 3 centimeters -1 1/4 inches from the base of the artichokes. Cut off the base of the leaves, while turning the artichokes, and peel the stem. Finally, cut off the tops of the leaves. As they are prepared, set them aside in water to which the lemon juice is added.

Combine 2 liters - 8 1/2 cups water with the wine in a saucepan and bring to a boil. Immerse the artichokes for 30 seconds to blanch them, then drain in a colander.

Assemble the artichokes in oil
Separate the garlic cloves. Pack the artichoke hearts in a sterilized jar, and as you do so, insert the garlic cloves, bay leaves, peppercorns, and juniper berries in the spaces between them. Pour in the olive oil to within 1 centimeter - 1/2 inch from the rim of the jar. Close tightly.

AD - Take full advantage of the poivrade (or purple) artichoke season, when they're inexpensive, to preserve them this way.

PN - These poivrade artichokes will make delicious antipasti in winter, as a change from grated carrots.

PRESERVED FAIRY RING MUSHROOMS

MAKES ENOUGH TO FILL ONE 500-MILLILITER - 16.9-FLUID-OUNCE JAR
PREPARATION TIME: 30 MINUTES
COOK TIME: 20 MINUTES

500 grams - 1 pound 2 ounces mushrooms, preferably fairy ring
250 milliliters - 1 cup white wine vinegar
1 sprig rosemary
2 sprigs thyme
2 cloves garlic
Salt
500 milliliters - 2 cups olive oil

AD - This recipe can actually be used for any kind of mushroom. Take advantage of them in any season; it's so fast and easy.

PN - It's also very practical to have those mushrooms at hand to make an omelet when you don't have time to shop for your dinner.

Sterilize the jar
Bring water to a boil in a large cast-iron pot or a stock-pot. Put the jar and the lid in the pot and boil for 20 minutes. Let the jar cool inside the pan.

Prepare the mushrooms
Cut off the base of the stems, then wash the mushrooms quickly without soaking them. Drain and gently dry with a cloth.

Assemble the preserved mushrooms
In a saucepan, combine 1 liter - 4 1/4 cups water with the vinegar, rosemary, thyme, peeled garlic, and 3 pinches of salt and bring to a boil. Immerse the mushrooms for 5 minutes. Using a skimmer, transfer to a tray lined with paper towels.

Put the mushrooms in the jar, inserting the sprigs of rosemary and thyme, and the garlic cloves between them. Tap the jar often to compact the mushrooms. Then pour the oil into the jar to completely cover the mushrooms. Close tightly. Store immediately in a cool and dry place away from light.

ALMONDS

APRICOTS

CHERRIES

FIGS

LEMONS

MELONS

PEACHES

PLUMS

RASPBERRIES

ARTICHOKES

BROCCOLI

CELERY

CHARD

CUCUMBERS

EGGPLANT

FENNEL

GARLIC

GREEN BEANS

ONIONS

PEPPERS

PORCINI MUSHROOMS

POTATOES

TOMATOES

ZUCCHINI

SUMMER

MARINATED SEA HERB CONDIMENT

SERVES 4
PREPARATION TIME: 30 MINUTES
COOK TIME: 20 MINUTES

200 grams - 7 ounces samphire or sea aster (or seaweed)
100 grams - 3 1/2 ounces sea lettuce, salt removed
1 anchovy fillet
2 tablespoons shallot vinaigrette (see p. 116)
Juice of 1/2 lemon
100 milliliters - 1/3 cup plus 1 tablespoon olive oil
Salt
Pepper
Fresh horseradish

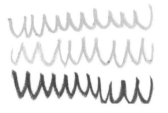

Prepare the samphire (or sea aster) and sea lettuce
Immerse the samphire in a bowl filled with cold water and rinse well. Strain. Do the same with the sea letttuce.

Make the condiment
Combine the samphire (or sea aster) and sea lettuce in a blender. Cut the anchovy fillet into small pieces and add to the blender with the shallot vinaigrette and lemon juice.
Blend while gradually adding the olive oil, until the mixture is smooth. Season with salt and pepper.
Peel the horseradish root, grate, and add to the condiment, adjusting the amount to your taste.

AD - Here's a perfect sauce for seasoning a poached fish or steamed vegetables. It makes a great substitute for aïoli, when you feel like a change and want to surprise your guests.

PN - This sauce is packed with vitamins and minerals. Samphire and sea aster aren't seaweed but actually small fleshy plants that grow in salt marshes. They have practically the same nutritional content as seaweed, seeing as they grow in seawater.

CILANTRO CONDIMENT

SERVES 4
PREPARATION TIME: 30 MINUTES
COOK TIME: 20 MINUTES

6 shallots
300 milliliters - 1 1/4 cups aged wine vinegar
2 bunches cilantro (coriander)
300 milliliters - 1 1/4 cups olive oil
Salt
Freshly ground pepper

Make the pickled shallots
Peel and mince the shallots. Put in a saucepan, add the vinegar, and simmer over low heat until they are soft and all the vinegar has evaporated, about 20 minutes. Transfer to a bowl and refrigerate.

Make the condiment
Wash, dry, and pluck the cilantro leaves. Coarsely chop the leaves and put them in a blender. Add the pickled shallots and blend, while gradually adding the olive oil, until the mixture is smooth. Season with salt and pepper. Transfer the condiment to a bowl and refrigerate until ready to use.

AD – If you're worried about the quite strong and particular flavor of the cilantro, tone it down with some parsley by using a bunch of each.

PN – In any case, both are really high in vitamins and minerals. They're also chock-full of antioxidants, as are the shallots. This condiment is really good for your health.

EGGPLANT MAYONNAISE

SERVES 4
PREPARATION TIME: 15 MINUTES
COOK TIME: 1 HOUR

1 large or 2 medium eggplants
(aubergines)
1 egg yolk
1 teaspoon mustard
1 tablespoon labneh (Lebanese
cream cheese) or plain Greek
yogurt
Salt
Espelette pepper

Prepare the eggplant
Preheat the oven to 180°C - 350°F (gas mark 4).
Wash, dry, and halve the eggplants. Prick the flesh all over with a fork and wrap each half in aluminum foil. Bake in the oven for 1 hour.
Remove from the oven and let cool slightly. Then use a teaspoon to scoop out the flesh into a small bowl. Weigh the flesh. You need 250 grams - 9 ounces.

Make the eggplant mayonnaise
Mix the egg yolk with the mustard in a bowl. Add the labneh and mix well. Pour this mixture into the bowl with the eggplant and mix well. Season with salt.
Transfer to another bowl and sprinkle with a little Espelette pepper. Cover the bowl with plastic wrap (cling film) and refrigerate until ready to serve.

AD - If you can't find labneh, the Lebanese cream cheese, make it yourself. Mix the contents of one container of yogurt with a good pinch of salt. Put it in a strainer lined with cheesecloth or muslin and let it drain in the refrigerator for at least eight hours.

PN - You might want to make it with several cups of yogurt, given the time it takes to make. This labneh is useful and can accompany crudités. I love this eggplant mayonnaise; it's super light and has lots of calcium

ZUCCHINI AND NEW GARLIC SOUP

SERVES 4
PREPARATION TIME: 15 MINUTES
COOK TIME: 6 MINUTES
CHILL TIME: 2 HOURS

5 trumpet zucchini
(courgettes)
10 cloves new garlic
100 milliliters - 1/3 cup
plus 1 tablespoon olive oil,
plus more for drizzling
1 liter - 4 1/4 cups almond
milk
Salt
1 sprig mint
Freshly ground pepper

AD - If you can't find any trumpet zucchini, use other varieties, but choose small ones. Typically, there isn't a green core (germ) to remove in new garlic. This develops gradually as the garlic gets older.

PN - It's a shame to have to remove the green core from garlic, because its beneficial compounds, allicin among them, are concentrated there. Allicin is the cause of the dreaded, smelly belching. But when garlic is cooked, it loses its strength. So you can keep the green core; it's better for your health.

Prepare the zucchini and garlic
Wash the zucchini. Dry them and cut off the ends. Leave unpeeled. Cut into slices and put in a bowl. Peel and halve the garlic cloves. Add them to the bowl.

Heat 2 tablespoons of olive oil in a cast-iron pot or Dutch oven and brown the zucchini and garlic for 2-3 minutes.

Add the almond milk, mix well, and cook for 3 minutes.

Prepare a bowl filled with water and plenty of ice cubes. Transfer the zucchini mixture to another, slightly smaller, bowl and put it over the bowl with water and ice cubes. Stir the mixture to cool.

Make the soup
Use a handheld immersion blender to blend the soup until perfectly smooth. Add the remaining oil and blend again. Season with salt and pepper and blend again.

Discard the water and ice cubes. Place a conical strainer over the chilled bowl and filter the soup through it. Refrigerate for at least 2 hours. Also chill four serving bowls.

Finish and serve
Rinse, dry, and pluck the mint. Pour the soup into the chilled serving bowls, then scatter the mint leaves over the soup. Drizzle with a little olive oil and serve.

MELON, PORT, GINGER, AND HERBS

SERVES 4
PREPARATION TIME: 15 MINUTES
COOK TIME: 10 MINUTES

200 milliliters - 3/4 cup
plus 1 tablespoon port
2 pinches Espelette pepper
2 cantaloupes
5-centimeter- - 2-inch-length
ginger
2 sprigs flat-leaf parsley
2 sprigs mint
2 sprigs basil
2 sprigs chervil
1 tablespoon olive oil
Juice of 1 lemon
Fleur de sel

Make the port syrup
Put the port in a saucepan and add the Espelette pepper. Mix and bring to a boil. Lower the heat and cook until the port is reduced to a syrup, about 10 minutes.

Prepare the fruit and ginger
Halve both cantaloupes and remove all of the seeds. Use a large knife to remove all of the skin. Cut the flesh into 3-centimeter - 1 1/4-inch cubes, transfer to a large dish, and refrigerate. Peel and cut the ginger into small batons. Set aside.

Prepare the herbs
Rinse, dry, and pluck the parsley, mint, basil, and chervil leaves. Put all of the herbs in a bowl. Add the olive oil, lemon juice, and a pinch of fleur de sel.

Finish and serve
When it is time to serve, pour the port syrup over the melon cubes and mix gently. Add the ginger and herbs, then serve.

AD - You can try variations of this dish using Madeira or even a sweet wine such as muscatel. The melons have to be very ripe, naturally.

PN - It's often like a lottery, finding out how ripe a melon is. Check the stem carefully. If it's about to fall off, the melon is quite ripe. If there's a little drop of cantaloupe juice there, that's even better.

ZUCCHINI SALAD WITH LEMON

SERVES 4
PREPARATION TIME: 30 MINUTES
COOK TIME: 1 HOUR 6 MINUTES

4 organic, unwaxed lemons
2 tablespoons honey
30 grams - 1 ounce/1/4 cup
currants
500 grams - 1 pound 2 ounces
small zucchini
1 red onion
2 zucchini flowers
1 clove garlic
30 grams - 1 ounce/1/4 cup
pine nuts
Olive oil
Salt
Espelette pepper

AD - These candied lemon rinds have quite a kick to them. You can make a large amount and keep them easily in their juice in a well-sealed jar in the fridge.

PN - What a copious salad. It serves as a hearty vegetable dish to accompany a cold meat.

Prepare the lemon

Cut 2 lemons into ten sections (segments) each. Use a paring knife to separate the flesh from the rind by passing the blade between the flesh and the pith (the white skin attached to the yellow rind). Place the pieces of rind in a saucepan. Then squeeze the pulp sections with your fingers into the pan. Squeeze the juice of the other 2 lemons and add it to the pan together with the honey. Simmer for 1 hour until the lemon rinds are very soft and candied. Transfer to a bowl and refrigerate.

Prepare the vegetables

Soak the currants in a bowl filled with warm water. Wash the zucchini and cut into thick rounds. Peel the onion and slice into thin rounds. Remove and discard the pistil from the zucchini flowers; shred the flowers. Peel and finely slice the garlic. Heat a little olive oil in a sauté pan. Sauté the zucchini and onion for about 5 minutes, keeping them slightly firm. Drain the currants and add them to the pan. Add the zucchini flowers and the garlic slices. Cook for only 1 minute, then transfer to a salad bowl.

Finish the salad

Heat a dry nonstick frying pan and toast the pine nuts. Drain on paper towels. Drain the candied lemon rinds and add them to the vegetables in the bowl. Add 4 tablespoons olive oil to the remaining juice and beat well with a fork to make an emulsion. Season with salt and pepper. Pour this dressing into the bowl and mix well. Arrange the salad on plates. Scatter with toasted pine nuts. Serve cold.

CHARD, TOMATOES, AND ANCHOVIES

SERVES 4
PREPARATION TIME: 15 MINUTES
COOK TIME: 30 MINUTES

2 bunches thin-stemmed Swiss chard
4 very ripe tomatoes
2 Welsh onions or scallions
2 cloves garlic
8 anchovy fillets in oil
30 grams - 1 ounce / 2 tablespoons butter
Salt
Olive oil
30 grams - 1 ounce / 1/3 cup grated Parmesan cheese

AD – Don't throw away the Welsh onion leaves. Save them for a soup. They are too tough to be pleasant eaten raw, but they're perfect cooked.

PN – This dish is very Mediterranean, chef, and especially from Nice. In the Nice region there's a real devotion to Swiss chard, even to the point where a sweet tart is made from it.

Prepare the vegetables
Wash and dry the chard well, then separate the stems from the leaves. Remove the strings from the leaves, and set aside the leaves and stems separately. Wash and dry the tomatoes. Halve them, then cut into about 4-millimeter - 1/8-inch-thick slices. Peel off the outer layer of skin from the Welsh onions, cut off the tough leaves, and cut the white part into small diagonal slices. Peel the garlic cloves; crush one clove.

Cook the chard and tomatoes
Cut the anchovy fillets into small pieces. Gently heat the butter in a large cast-iron pan. When it becomes frothy, add the anchovies and dissolve them over very low heat for 2 minutes. Add the chard stems, Welsh onion slices, and the crushed garlic clove. Season lightly with salt. Cover with a lid and cook over low heat for 10 minutes, then add about 50 milliliters - 2 1/2 tablespoons water,

stir, and cook for about 5 minutes. Take off the lid and reduce the cooking liquid until it is syrupy. Mix. The stems should be bound well and coated in the liquid.

Cook the chard leaves
Prick the other garlic clove with a fork and leave it on the end. Heat a little olive oil in a sauté pan, add the chard leaves, and stir with the garlic clove on the end of the fork until they wilt (approximately 2-3 minutes).

Finish and serve
Preheat the oven to 180°C - 350°F (gas mark 4). Arrange the chard leaves, stems mixed with Welsh onions, and the raw tomato slices in an ovenproof dish. Drizzle with the chard stem cooking liquid remaining in the pan. Sprinkle lightly with Parmesan and bake for 15 minutes. Serve immediately in the dish.

BROCCOLI AND CLAMS

1 kilogram - 2 pounds 4 ounces clams
Salt
1 head broccoli, about 600 grams - 1 pound 5 ounces
1 shallot
1 clove garlic
Olive oil
10 black peppercorns, plus freshly ground pepper
1/2 bunch flat-leaf parsley
250 milliliters - 1 cup white wine
1/2 organic, unwaxed lemon
1 tablespoon flour

Clean the clams several hours ahead
Soak the clams in a large bowl filled with heavily salted water. Refrigerate for 8 hours to let them expel all of their grit. Then, rinse several times in clean water to remove the grit.

Prepare the broccoli
Cut the broccoli into florets and wash (save the stems for a soup). Bring very lightly salted water to a boil in a saucepan and prepare a bowl with water and ice cubes. Immerse the florets in the boiling water for 3 minutes, then remove with a skimmer and shock in the ice water. Drain and dry them.

Prepare the clams
Peel and mince the shallot; crush the garlic clove. Heat a little olive oil in a sauté pan with the shallot, garlic clove, peppercorns, and 1 sprig parsley. Drain the clams and add them

to the pan. Mix well. Add the white wine and mix again. Remove the clams from the pan as they open and transfer to a bowl. Strain the cooking liquid through a conical strainer into another small bowl. Set aside.

Finish and serve
Cut the lemon half into a small dice. Wash, dry, pluck, and mince the remaining parsley leaves. Remove all of the clams from their shells. Heat 1 tablespoon of olive oil with the flour in a cast-iron pan. Mix and cook for 2 minutes. Deglaze with the reserved clam cooking liquid, mix, and simmer until the liquid thickens into a sauce, 2-3 minutes. Add the clams and the broccoli. Gently mix. Season with salt and pepper. Add the diced lemon and minced parsley. Stir carefully. Serve the clams and broccoli on individual plates or in a large serving dish.

BRAISED GUINEA FOWL WITH PEACHES

SERVES 4
PREPARATION TIME: 15 MINUTES
COOK TIME: 45 MINUTES

1 guinea fowl, cleaned
8 yellow peaches
1 shallot
Olive oil
Salt
100 milliliters - 1/3 cup
plus 1 tablespoon chicken
broth
1 handful green almonds
2 sprigs verbena
2 tablespoons crème fraîche
Freshly ground pepper

AD – This combination of guinea fowl and peaches is unusual. It was a great idea by Christophe Saintagne and it works really well. Take care not to overcook the peaches or you'll end up with a compote.

PN – That's why it's better to use yellow peaches, which have much firmer flesh than white peaches. Also, they contain more antioxidant carotenoids than white peaches.

Prepare the guinea fowl and the peaches
Cut the guinea fowl into eight pieces, or have your butcher do this.

Blanch the peaches in boiling water for 30 seconds, then peel, remove the pit (stone), and quarter them. Peel and mince the shallot.

Make the braised guinea fowl with peaches
Heat a little olive oil in a cast-iron pan over medium heat. Brown the guinea fowl pieces on all sides, about 5 minutes total. Drain on paper towels.

Put the shallot in the pan and sweat over medium heat while stirring constantly. Return the guinea fowl to the pan, season with salt, and add the chicken broth. Cook over medium heat for 30 minutes.

Add the peaches to the pan. Cover with a lid and cook for 5 minutes. Gently turn the fruit pieces over and cook for 5 minutes more.

Finish and serve
While the guinea fowl is cooking, peel the green almonds. Halve them lengthwise and set aside on a plate. Rinse, dry, and pluck the verbena.

Remove the guinea fowl and peaches from the pan. Transfer to a warm serving dish. Add the crème fraîche to the pan and melt, while scraping the caramelized juices from the bottom of the pan. Add the almonds and the verbena. Check and adjust the salt, and season generously with pepper. Pour the sauce over the guinea fowl and peaches.

SUMMER VEGETABLE CROQUE-MADAME

SERVES 4
PREPARATION TIME: 15 MINUTES
COOK TIME: 40 MINUTES

1 red bell pepper
1 fennel bulb
1 zucchini
1 eggplant
Salt
Olive oil
Espelette pepper
1 tomato
1 romaine lettuce heart
1 clove garlic
2 sprigs small-leaf basil
8 slices sandwich bread
4 eggs
Freshly ground pepper

Prepare the vegetables
Preheat the oven to 150°C - 300°F (gas mark 2).
Peel, wash, deseed, and cut the bell pepper into eight uniform slices. Peel and wash the fennel, zucchini, and eggplant, and cut into 3-millimeter - 1/8-inch-thick slices.

Spread out the vegetables in a baking dish or on a baking sheet and season with salt. Drizzle with 4 tablespoons olive oil and sprinkle with a little Espelette pepper. Cook in the oven for 20 minutes.

Prepare the tomato, lettuce, and bread
In the meantime, wash, dry, and slice the tomato. Separate and wash the lettuce leaves. Peel the garlic clove. Wash, dry, and pluck the basil leaves.

Toast the bread, then rub with garlic.

Make the croque-madames
Lay out 4 slices of toast. Cover them with the cooked pepper, fennel, zucchini, and eggplant, and the tomato slices. Finish with the lettuce and basil leaves.

Cover with another slice of toast. Press lightly, then keep in place with a small wooden skewer. Arrange the croque-madames on plates.

Heat a splash of olive oil in a small nonstick frying pan. Break an egg into it and cook until the white sets. Slide it onto a croque-madame. Do the same for the remaining 3 eggs. Season lightly with salt, sprinkle generously with pepper, and serve.

AD - This vegetable croque-madame can actually be made year-round; you just have to adapt it to the vegetables in season. It can also be transformed into a burger made with good buns (see p. 366).

PN - I think this is a very practical dinner. It's also a good way to get people who don't like vegetables-children and grown-ups alike-to eat them.

RABBIT, CELERIAC, TOMATO, AND OLIVES

SERVES 4
PREPARATION TIME: 20 MINUTES
COOK TIME: 35 MINUTES

400 grams - 14 ounces
celeriac
Juice of 1/2 lemon, plus
juice of 1 lemon
1 egg yolk
1 tablespoon mustard
1 (150-gram - 5.3-ounce)
container plain (natural)
yogurt
1 tablespoon sherry vinegar
Salt
Freshly ground pepper
4 rabbit forequarters
Olive oil
300 milliliters - 1 1/4 cups
chicken broth
24 petals tomato confit (see
p. 363)
200 grams - 7 ounces/2 cups
small Nice olives
1/2 bunch flat-leaf parsley

AD - Buy a free-range rabbit, not a battery rabbit, which has been reared in terrible conditions and whose meat is soft. Don't hesitate to ask your butcher what kind of rabbit it is.

PN - Ah . . . I love this mayonnaise-free remoulade. A celeriac remoulade that isn't loaded with calories. Thanks for creating it. It can be served on its own as an appetizer, to take the edge off your hunger and so you eat less afterward.

Make the celeriac remoulade
Preheat the oven to 160°C - 325°F (gas mark 3).
Peel and grate the celeriac, but not too finely. Put in a bowl, drizzle with the juice of the 1/2 lemon, and mix well to prevent the celeriac from turning black.

Combine the egg yolk, mustard, and yogurt in a bowl and mix. Add the vinegar, mix again, and season with salt and pepper. Pour this remoulade over the celeriac. Mix and refrigerate until ready to serve.

Prepare the rabbit
Separate the legs from the rib cages, then cut the rib cages into two pieces. Season with salt.

Heat a little olive oil in a sauté pan and brown the rabbit on all sides.

When golden, transfer the pieces to an ovenproof dish and add the chicken broth and the juice of 1 lemon. Cook in the oven for 20 minutes.

Add the tomato confit and olives, baste generously with the cooking liquid, and return to the oven for another 10 minutes.

Finish and serve
Wash, dry, pluck, and chop the parsley leaves. Take the dish out of the oven. Add the parsley and gently mix. Serve the rabbit in the dish or on individual plates. Serve the celeriac remoulade alongside.

MACKEREL, APRICOT, AND LIME

SERVES 4
PREPARATION TIME: 15 MINUTES
COOK TIME: 5 MINUTES
REST TIME: 8 HOURS

8 young mackerel
Salt
Olive oil
Superfine (caster) sugar
12 medium or 8 large apricots
2 organic, unwaxed limes
1/2 bunch flat-leaf parsley
50 milliliters - 3 1/2
tablespoons white wine
1 tablespoon crème fraîche
Freshly ground pepper

AD – The French term for young mackerel, lisette, is probably derived from luisette, which comes from the verb luire, meaning "to gleam," an appropriate description of the shiny skin of mackerel.

PN – Mackerel and lisettes are very good, filled with beneficial fatty acids and omega-3. Apricots contain a lot of antioxidant carotenoids. All of these are excellent for your health.

Prepare the fish several hours ahead
Ask the fishmonger to fillet and debone the mackerel. Weigh your fillets and put them in a dish. Prepare a mixture of 18 grams - 1 tablespoon salt and 2 grams - 1/2 teaspoon sugar for every 1 kilogram - 2 pounds 2 ounces of fillets. Cover the fillets with this salt-sugar mixture and refrigerate for 8 hours.

Cook the fish
Heat a little olive oil in a frying pan and sear the fillets skin side down for 20 seconds. Transfer to a dish and keep hot.

Prepare the apricots, lemons, and parsley
Wash, dry, and remove the pits (stones) from the apricots. Peel 1 lime and cut the flesh into a small dice. Set aside. Rinse, dry, and pluck the parsley leaves. Chop the leaves and set aside in a bowl. Heat 1 tablespoon olive oil in a nonstick frying pan. Add the apricots and diced lime and shake the pan briskly for 3–4 minutes.

Finish and serve
Arrange the apricots on serving plates (or in a serving dish) and keep hot. Deglaze the pan with the white wine and reduce a little. Add the crème fraîche and stir well. Grate a little lime zest over the sauce. Then squeeze the lime over the sauce. Stir, check the taste, and adjust the seasoning with salt and pepper. Finish by adding the chopped parsley. Arrange the fish over the apricots. Cover with the sauce. Serve hot.

PIGEON, CHERRIES, AND YELLOW BELL PEPPERS

SERVES 4
PREPARATION TIME: 30 MINUTES
COOK TIME: 27 MINUTES

2 pigeons
2 yellow bell peppers
1 white onion
200 grams - 7 ounces/1 1/2 cups cherries
100 grams - 3 1/2 ounces sun-dried tomatoes
Olive oil
5 juniper berries
2 cloves new garlic
1 sprig thyme
1 sprig rosemary
150 milliliters - 2 1/3 cups chicken broth (see p. 62)
3 sprigs flat-leaf parsley
Salt
Freshly ground pepper

Prepare the pigeons
Singe the pigeon to remove any feathers and clean them. Separate the legs from the breasts, but leave them attached to each other. Tie up each pair of legs with kitchen twine. Tie up the breasts. You can also have your butcher do this for you.

Prepare the vegetables and cherries
Peel the peppers with a vegetable peeler. Cut into 3-millimeter - 1/8-inch-wide strips. Spread them out in an ovenproof baking dish. Peel and mince the onion. Add it to the dish. Remove the stems from the cherries, then halve and pit them. Add them to the dish together with the sun-dried tomatoes. Drizzle with 2 tablespoons olive oil and toss.

AD - This dish can also be made using quails. But they have to be good-quality ones, not industrially reared ones whose meat resembles cotton. And cook them whole.

PN - Pigeon has great merit; its meat is particularly high in iron. And it's also lean. This is a real dieter's dish you've invented for us.

Cook the pigeons and the vegetables
Preheat the oven to 220°C - 425°F (gas mark 7). Put the breasts, skin side up, and the legs over the vegetables and cherries, then cook in the oven for 12 minutes. Take the dish out of the oven and transfer the breasts to a plate and cover with aluminum foil. Crush the juniper berries and add them to the baking dish, along with the whole garlic cloves, the thyme, and the rosemary. Lower the oven temperature to 170°C - 340°F (gas mark 3–4) and return to the oven for 10 minutes. Moisten with the chicken broth and cook for another 5 minutes. Take the dish out of the oven and rest for 5 minutes.

Finish and serve
Rinse, dry, pluck, and chop the parsley leaves. Untie the breasts and halve them. Untie the legs. Gently mix to bind the vegetables and cherries well. Add the parsley and mix. Arrange the pigeon breast pieces and legs on the dish, then serve.

BELL PEPPERS AND MARINATED ANCHOVIES

SERVES 6
PREPARATION TIME: 20 MINUTES
CHILL TIME: 12 HOURS

500 grams - 1 pound 2 ounces
fresh anchovies
2 handfuls coarse sea salt
2 red bell peppers
2 cloves new garlic
1 sprig savory
1 sprig thyme
1 sprig rosemary
1 teaspoon Espelette pepper
4 tablespoons olive oil
Juice of 1 lemon
1 bunch flat-leaf parsley

AD - This recipe works very well with sardines, too. The salt cooks the fish, which have to be absolutely fresh, of course.

PN - Serve these anchovies with slices of whole-wheat toast. They'll be even better and you'll also have slow-release carbohydrate and dietary fiber. Between the peppers and parsley, you'll pretty much have your daily dose of vitamin C and antioxidants covered.

Prepare the anchovies
Rinse the anchovies well and fillet them, or have your fishmonger do it for you. Make a layer of coarse salt on a tray and lay the fillets out flat, skin side down. Marinate for 10 minutes.

Prepare the peppers, herbs, and garlic
In the meantime, peel the peppers with a vegetable peeler. Cut each one in half. Carefully remove the seeds and white ribs, then cut each half into thin strips.

Peel and mince the garlic cloves. Rinse, dry, and pluck the savory, thyme, and rosemary leaves, collecting them in a small bowl with the garlic. Mix with the Espelette pepper.

Prepare the peppers and marinated anchovies
Transfer the anchovy fillets from the salt to a paper towel. Place another sheet of paper towel over them and pat lightly to absorb the moisture.

On a serving platter, alternate anchovy fillets with strips of bell pepper. Sprinkle with the herb and garlic mixture. Drizzle with olive oil and the lemon juice. Refrigerate, covered, for 12 hours.

Finish and serve
Before serving, rinse, dry, pluck, and mince the parsley leaves and scatter them over the anchovies and peppers. Serve immediately.

SUMMER VEGETABLE AND LAMB TAGINE

SERVES 4-6
PREPARATION TIME: 30 MINUTES
COOK TIME: 1 HOUR 10 MINUTES
REST TIME: 2 HOURS

500 grams - 1 pound 2 ounces lamb shoulder, deboned
1 preserved lemon (see p. 200)
2 cloves new garlic
Olive oil
1 pinch saffron
1 teaspoon ground ginger
Salt
Freshly ground pepper
1 kilogram - 2 pounds 4 ounces young peas, unshelled
4 purple artichokes
Juice of 1 lemon
3 red onions
1 small head broccoli
2 handfuls snow peas
2 yellow bell peppers
2 Chioggia beets
500 milliliters - 2 cups chicken broth (see p. 62)
8 petals tomato confit (see p. 363)

Marinate the lamb

Remove the fat from the lamb. Quarter the preserved lemon. Crush the garlic cloves. Pour 2 tablespoons olive oil in a dish. Add the saffron, ginger, the pulp from the preserved lemon (set aside the rind), crushed garlic cloves, and some salt and pepper. Add the lamb pieces and mix. Cover with plastic wrap (cling film) and marinate for 2 hours at room temperature.

Prepare the vegetables

Shell the peas. Turn the artichokes by paring the base to remove the largest leaves, quarter, remove the choke, and immerse in water with the lemon juice. Peel the onions and slice into thick strips. Wash the broccoli and cut off the florets. Wash and remove the strings from the snow peas. Rinse the bell peppers and cut into 8 pieces. Peel the beets and cut into pieces.

Prepare the tajine

Heat the tajine pot. Put a little olive oil in the pot and add the artichokes, onions, and peppers. Cover with the lid and cook for 4 minutes. Transfer the vegetables to a dish and cover with aluminum foil. Drain the lamb pieces and put them in the tajine pot. Brown on all sides for 10 minutes. Add the marinade and 1 ladle of chicken broth, then add the beets. Simmer for 45 minutes, gradually adding broth. The lamb should never be totally immersed.

Cook the green vegetables

Bring a saucepan of salted water to a boil and prepare a bowl with water and ice cubes. Immerse the broccoli florets, peas, and snow peas in the boiling water for 4 minutes, then shock in the ice water. Drain.

Finish and serve

After the lamb cooks for 45 minutes, add the artichokes, onions, peppers, and the preserved lemon rind. Cook for another 15 minutes, adding a little broth if necessary. Add the broccoli, peas, snow peas, and tomato confit petals. Cook for a further 3 minutes. Check and adjust the seasoning. Serve in the tajine pot.

TARTARE OF VEAL, WHITE PEACHES, AND GREEN BEANS

SERVES 4
PREPARATION TIME: 30 MINUTES
COOK TIME: 6 MINUTES

400 grams - 14 ounces green
beans
Salt
400 grams - 14 ounces cushion
of milk-fed veal
1/2 bunch flat-leaf parsley
1/2 bunch chervil
1/2 bunch chives
Freshly ground pepper
8 green almonds
2 white peaches
4 tablespoons olive oil
Juice of 2 limes

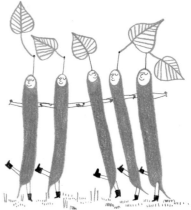

AD - Cut the veal with a knife; never use a grinder (mincer) or you'll end up with a mush and not a tartare. If you take everything out of the refrigerator 30 minutes before plating and serving, this tartare will be even better.

Prepare the green beans
Remove the strings, wash, and halve the beans while heating a saucepan of salted water. Immerse in the boiling water for 6 minutes. Meanwhile, fill a bowl with cold water and ice cubes. Drain the beans and immediately shock in the ice water. Drain the beans and set aside in the refrigerator.

Cube the veal
Cut the veal into about 4-millimeter - 1/8-inch cubes (or have your butcher do this for you). Put in a bowl and refrigerate.

Prepare the herbs and fruits
Wash and dry the parsley, chervil and chives. Pluck the parsley and chervil leaves, then mince them and the chives. Set half aside and

add the remainder to the veal. Season the veal with salt and pepper.

Peel and cut the almonds into small pieces.

Peel the peaches, remove the pit (stone), and cut into slices.

Finish and serve
Season the veal with 2 tablespoons olive oil, the juice of the limes, salt, and freshly ground pepper. Season the green beans with the reserved herbs and the remaining olive oil.

Put some veal and green beans on individual plates and toss gently. Scatter with almonds and peach slices. Season with pepper and serve.

VEGGIE BURGER

1 eggplant
1/2 red onion
2 cloves garlic
1/4 bunch cilantro
Olive oil
Salt
1 sprig thyme
2 or 3 drops hot sauce
1 beefsteak tomato
1 zucchini
Flour
Freshly ground pepper
1/2 red onion
1 head Little Gem lettuce
Burger buns (see p. 366)

Make the buns (p. 366)

Make the eggplant condiment
Wash, dry, and cut the eggplant in half. Set aside one half, then chop the other half into a 1-centimeter - 1/2-inch dice. Peel and mince the onion half and 1 of the garlic cloves. Wash, dry, pluck, and mince the cilantro leaves.

AC - To save time, bake the buns or make the dough the previous day. And don't even think about using store-bought burger buns, which are bland, boring, and contain too much sugar.

PN - Vegans will love you for this recipe, chef. It's full of vitamins, minerals, and dietary fiber thanks to the vegetables. And it's good for everyone, including children.

Heat a little olive oil in a frying pan and sweat the onion and garlic without coloring for 2–3 minutes. Add the diced eggplant and thyme, and season very lightly with salt. Cook for 2–3 minutes, then transfer to a bowl. Let cool, then add the cilantro and 2–3 drops of hot sauce.

Prepare the sliced, fried vegetables
Wash the tomato, and zucchini, then cut these vegetables, and the other eggplant half, into 1-centimeter- - 1/2-inch-thick slices. Dredge the slices lightly in flour. Heat 2 tablespoons olive oil in a large frying pan and brown the slices for 1 minute on each side. Season with salt and pepper.

Make the burgers
Cut the onion half into thin slices. Wash and dry the lettuce head, separate the leaves, and finely slice. Heat the oven to 160°C - 325°F (gas mark 3) and reheat the burger buns for 10 minutes. Cut the remaining garlic clove in half. Cut each bun in half across the middle and rub with the garlic. Spread each bottom half with eggplant condiment, then cover this with the vegetable slices, alternating the different vegetables. Finish with the onion and shredded sucrine lettuce. Cover with the top half of the buns and serve.

EINKORN, FENNEL, AND RAISINS

SERVES 4
PREPARATION TIME: 5 MINUTES
COOK TIME: 25 MINUTES

30 grams - 1 ounce/3 1/2 tablespoons raisins
1 white onion
800 milliliters - 3 1/3 cups chicken broth (see p. 62)
10 grams - 3/8 ounce/2 teaspoons butter
Olive oil
200 grams - 7 ounces/1 cup einkorn wheat berries
2 young fennel bulbs
Salt
Freshly ground pepper

Prepare the raisins
Soak the raisins in a bowl of hot water.

Cook the einkorn
Peel and mince the onion. Put the chicken broth in a saucepan and place over the heat. Bring to a boil.
Heat the butter with 2 tablespoons olive oil in a deep frying pan. Add the minced onion and sweat for 5 minutes while stirring constantly. Add the einkorn and stir for 2–3 minutes.

Pour in a ladle of boiling broth. Stir and let it be absorbed by the einkorn. Next, add the broth, one ladle at a time. Wait for the broth to be absorbed before adding the next ladle (as if cooking risotto). Cook this way until the einkorn becomes soft, about 20 minutes.

Prepare the fennel
While the einkorn is cooking, wash and dry the fennel bulbs. Use a mandoline with safety guard to cut the fennel into thin slices.

Finish and serve
Add the fennel slices to the pan with the einkron. Mix well and cook for about 2 minutes. Drain the raisins, add them to the pan, and mix. Add a little broth if the mixture becomes too thick. Season with salt and pepper. Serve in the pan or on individual plates.

AD - This recipe uses einkorn from the Haute-Provence region, which is the only genuine einkorn.

PN - Einkorn is the ancestor of wheat. Interestingly, it is more often than not tolerated by people who are usually gluten-intolerant because it only contains about seven percent gluten. It contains more nutrients than wheat.

TOMATO AND RICOTTA LASAGNE

<u>SERVES 4</u>
<u>PREPARATION TIME: 5 MINUTES</u>
<u>COOK TIME: 45 MINUTES</u>

1/2 bunch flat-leaf parsley
1/2 bunch chervil
1/2 bunch basil
1/2 bunch chives
250 grams - 9 ounces/1 cup ricotta cheese
Olive oil
Salt
Freshly ground pepper
250 grams - 9 ounces lasagna sheets
300 grams - 10 1/2 ounces/1 1/4 cups tomato coulis (see p. 355)
32 petals tomato confit (see p. 363)
1 egg yolk
40 grams - 1 1/2 ounces/1/2 cup grated Parmesan cheese

AD - Ricotta is a fresh cheese made using the leftover whey from making other cheeses. Buy good Italian ricotta made from sheep's milk, not the industrially produced cow's milk ricotta you find in supermarkets.

PN - And if you find ricotta romana or ricotta di bufala campana (made from buffalo milk), both of which have PDO status, don't think twice about it. They're fantastic. Ricotta has lots of calcium; keep that in mind.

Make the herb ricotta
Wash, dry, pluck, and mince the parsley, chervil, and basil leaves. Wash, dry, and mince the chives. Put the ricotta in a bowl. Add the minced herbs and a little olive oil. Mix well. Check and adjust the seasoning with salt and pepper, and set aside.

Prepare the lasagna sheets
Bring a pot of salted water to a boil and prepare a bowl with water and ice cubes. Immerse the lasagna sheets in the boiling water for 30 seconds. Drain and immediately immerse in the ice water. Carefully dry between paper towels.

Assemble and cook the lasagna
Preheat the oven to 150°C - 300°F (gas mark 2).
Lightly grease an ovenproof dish with olive oil. Lay lasagna sheets over the bottom. Cover with a layer of tomato coulis about 8 millimeters - 1/3 inch thick. Lay 8 tomato confit petals over the coulis and add 8 teaspoons of the herb ricotta.

Repeat the same process three times to make four layers of pasta, finishing with a layer of tomato confit and herb ricotta.

Whisk the egg yolk with a splash of water in a bowl. Brush the surface uniformly with the egg. Then sprinkle with the Parmesan.

Bake for 40 minutes. Serve immediately.

RICE NOODLES, SUMMER PORCINI

SERVES 4
PREPARATION TIME: 15 MINUTES
COOK TIME: 10 MINUTES

300 grams - 10 1/2 ounces
fresh porcini mushrooms
1 clove garlic
1/2 bunch flat-leaf parsley
1/2 bunch cilantro
1 sweet red chili pepper
1 small red onion
1 tablespoon olive oil
Salt
250 grams - 9 ounces rice
noodles
Freshly ground pepper
Grated Parmesan cheese

Prepare the mushrooms
Clean the mushrooms well: Cut off the stems, then very quickly remove any remaining soil and leaves in water. Dry with a kitchen cloth or paper towels and cut into pieces. Peel and mince the garlic. Wash, dry, pluck, and mince the parsley and cilantro. Finely slice the chili into rings, chop the onion in slices. Heat the olive oil in a large sauté pan and sweat the mushrooms for about 5 minutes. Season with salt. Add the garlic, chili and onion, then cook for about 2 minutes more while stirring gently.

Prepare the rice noodles
In the meantime, cook the noodles in boiling salted water for the time indicated on the package.

Finish and serve
Drain the noodles. Add them to the pan and stir. Stir in the parsley and cilantro. Check and adjust the seasoning with salt and pepper. Serve the noodles on individual plates and pass the grated Parmesan separately.

AD - You can actually make this dish throughout the year using dried porcini mushrooms (about 80 grams - 2 3/4 ounces). Soak them in warm water for about 1 hour to rehydrate, then rinse three times in clean water.

PN - And if you don't want to use porcini mushrooms, this dish is suited to any mushrooms, including white ones. You can also use durum wheat noodles. This easy dish is high in carbohydrate and it has lots of vitamins, thanks to the herbs.

VEGETABLE-AND-BACON BREAD

500 grams - 1 pound 2 ounces young peas, unshelled
Salt
1 yellow or red bell pepper
1 red onion
100 grams - 3 1/2 ounces shiitake mushrooms
150 grams - 5 1/2 ounces smoked side (streaky) bacon
Freshly ground pepper
500 grams - 1 pound 2 ounces/4 cups flour, plus more for dusting
300 milliliters - 1 1/4 cups water
8 grams - 1/4 ounce active dry yeast

SERVES 4
PREPARATION TIME: 1 HOUR 45 MINUTES
COOK TIME: 30 MINUTES
REST TIME: 1 HOUR 30 MINUTES

AD - This bread is ideal for a snack. Serve it with the marinated marine herb condiment (see p. 280), the cilantro condiment (see p. 283), or the eggplant mayonnaise (see p. 284).

PN - This bread is practically a whole meal in itself. Carbohydrate, dietary fiber, vitamins, minerals, proteins—it has everything. And it's light, too, seeing that there's practically no fat. People on diets will love it.

Prepare the vegetables and bacon

Shell the peas. Bring a saucepan of salted water to a boil and prepare a bowl with water and ice cubes. Blanch the peas in the boiling water for 1 minute. Drain and shock in the ice water. Drain and set aside in a bowl. Wash and dry the pepper and cut into large pieces. Peel and finely slice the onion. Rinse and quarter the mushrooms. Add all of the vegetables to the bowl. Cut the bacon into 2-centimeter - 3/4-inch lardons.

Cook the vegetables

Heat a dry frying pan and add the lardons. Lower the heat a little and brown them. Add all of the vegetables, stir, and cook for 3 minutes while stirring constantly. Season with salt and pepper. Transfer to the bowl and let cool.

Make the bread

Combine the flour, water, and yeast in the bowl of a stand mixer fitted with a dough hook. Mix on low speed for 5 minutes. Dissolve 9 grams - 1/3 ounce/1 1/2 teaspoons salt in a little water and add. Mix for 5 more minutes. Stop the mixer and add the vegetables and bacon. Mix for another minute. Dust the work surface with flour and turn the dough out onto it. Shape into a 20-centimeter- - 7 3/4-inch-diameter ball. Transfer to a flour-dusted baking sheet, cover with a kitchen towel, and let rise (proof) for 1 hour 30 minutes at room temperature. Remove the kitchen towel.

Bake and serve the bread

Preheat the oven to 220°C - 425°F (gas mark 7). Put the baking sheet in the oven, lower the temperature to 180°C - 350°F (gas mark 4), and bake for about 20 minutes. When it comes out of the oven, immediately transfer the bread to a wire rack. Slice and serve.

SPAGHETTI WITH EGGPLANT AND SWORDFISH

SERVES 4
PREPARATION TIME: 15 MINUTES
COOK TIME: 15 MINUTES

2 eggplants (aubergines)
1 red onion
1 tomato
3 sprigs cilantro (coriander)
300 grams - 10 1/2 ounces
spaghetti
Salt
1 2-centimeter - 3/4-inch-
thick slice swordfish, about
150 grams - 5 1/2 ounces
Olive oil
Freshly ground pepper
1 organic, unwaxed lemon

Prepare the vegetables
Wash the eggplant and cut the flesh into a 1.5-centimeter - 5/8-inch dice. Peel and mince the onion. Peel and halve the tomato. Squeeze each half to remove the seeds and cut the flesh into a small dice. Wash, dry, and pluck the cilantro leaves.

Cook the spaghetti
Immerse the spaghetti in boiling salted water for the time indicated on the package.

Cook the fish and eggplant
Remove the skin from the fish and cut the flesh into 2-centimeter - 3/4-inch cubes. Heat 1 tablespoon olive oil in a frying pan and sauté the eggplant for 5 minutes. Season with salt and pepper, then transfer to a dish. Put a little more olive oil in the same pan and sauté the fish over high heat for 30 seconds, Season with salt and transfer to a separate dish.

Assemble the dish
Heat 1 tablespoon olive oil in a sauté pan. Sweat the onion for 3 minutes over medium heat without coloring. Add the cooked eggplant, the diced tomato, and the cilantro leaves, and mix gently. Drain the spaghetti and add to the pan. Mix well.

Finish and serve
At the last minute, add the swordfish to the pan. Mix gently. Grate the zest of the lemon over the top, add 1 tablespoon olive oil, and mix gently. Transfer the contents of the pan to a serving dish or arrange on individual plates.

AD - You can also serve this dish directly from the pan. This dish works with other kinds of fish, but always barely cooked; otherwise they'll turn to mush.

PN - This is a one-dish meal if ever there was one. It has everything: carbohydrate from the spaghetti and vegetables, and protein from the swordfish. Eat some yogurt and a piece of fruit afterward to round it off.

SUMMER VEGETABLE PIZZA

3 small spring (new) onions
3 cherry tomatoes
1 handful fairy ring mushrooms
1/2 head broccoli
Salt
1 small zucchini (courgette)
6 pitted black olives
1 small red bell pepper
3 tablespoons cream cheese
Espelette pepper
2 sprigs basil
1/2 clove garlic
1 batch pizza dough (see p. 367)
Olive oil
Fleur de sel

AD – If you can't find fairy ring mushrooms, simply use white mushrooms.

PN – There isn't an ounce of fat on your pizza, chef—just the one teaspoon of olive oil in the dough (see p. 367). This is absolutely low-fat, but really balanced at the same time, full of vitamins and minerals, and just the right amount of carbohydrate.

Prepare the pizza dough (p. 367)

Prepare the vegetables
Wash, dry, and peel the onions. Cut off the leaves (save for a soup), then slice 2 of the onions into rounds. Wash, dry, and quarter the tomatoes. Cut off the mushroom stems and wash and dry the caps. Wash and dry the broccoli and cut off the florets. Immerse the florets in boiling salted water for 3 minutes, then drain. Wash, dry, and shred the zucchini with a grater. Combine all of these vegetables in a bowl, add the olives, and mix.

Make the bell pepper cream cheese
Peel and finely slice the bell pepper. Slice the remaining onion and put in a blender. Add the pepper, 2 tablespoons of the cream cheese, a good pinch of Espelette pepper, and a pinch of salt. Blend until smooth.

Make the basil cream cheese
Rinse, pluck, and mince the basil leaves. Peel and chop the garlic half. Mix in a bowl with the rest of the cream cheese. Set aside.

Assemble and bake the pizza
Preheat the oven to 200°C - 400°F (gas mark 6). Roll out the pizza dough on the oven rack into a 4-millimeter - 1/8-inch-thick disk, then spread an even layer of the bell pepper cream cheese over it. Spread all of the vegetables over the pizza in an attractive arrangement. Bake for 10–15 minutes.

Finish and serve
Take the pizza out of the oven, sprinkle with a little Espelette pepper and fleur de sel, and add dollops of the basil cream cheese. Serve immediately.

A
P
R
I
C
O
T
S

The apricot's botanical name is *Prunus armeniaca,* the Armenium plum. It is nothing like a plum and, to tell the truth, did not originate in Armenia, although it was grown there in the first century BC. Like other fruits, it grew wild in China 4,000 to 6,000 years ago and gradually extended toward the Middle East. The name "apricot" was coined over the years, becoming *al barq* in Arabic. Introduced into Spain in the eighth century, it became *albaricoque* in Spanish and *alberoc* in Catalan. This led to the word *abricot,* when it finally arrived in France in the sixteenth century and was planted in the gardens of Versailles. King Louis XIV of France, a lover of sensuous indulgence, loved this juicy, fragrant, and round fruit, with a groove running down the middle that resembled a woman's buttocks. Apricots have always been eaten fresh, but also dried—under the sun in the past and in ovens today.

VARIETIES AND SEASONS

The apricot has a short growing season, beginning in late May and ending at the end of August. Favorite early harvesting varieties include the classic Blenheim, extra-large Royalty, sweet-tart Gold Kist, and mild Sungold. Goldcot, Hargrand, King, and Moorpark are all large, mid-season varieties, while Royal Rosa, Puget Gold, Montrose, and Golden Amber are popular late-harvesters.

CHOOSING AND STORAGE

Apricots can be bought from farmers' markets and specialty fruit and vegetable dealers who source their produce locally. The color of an apricot depends on its variety and is not a sign of quality. A ripe apricot has a very smooth skin, not downy. Its ripeness can be judged by pressing with a finger. It should be neither too soft nor too hard. It should be stored at room temperature. The kernel (pit) it encases contains a very small amount of a substance that can turn into cyanide, so it is best not to overdo it with the pits.

NUTRITION

Apricots, particularly dried apricots, are filled with protective antioxidant molecules of all kinds. They also contain dietary fiber and carbohydrate, but few vitamins.

USES AND COMBINATIONS

Apricots shine in pastry making (tarts, clafoutis, ice cream, etc.), but they are used less often in savory cuisine, except in dishes that combine sweet and savory. They go quite well with poultry, lamb, almonds, pistachios, and fresh goat cheese.

BRAISED FENNEL AND APRICOT

SERVES 4
PREPARATION TIME: 15 MINUTES
COOK TIME: 15 MINUTES

20 baby fennel bulbs
8 apricots
1 teaspoon coriander seeds
2 oranges
1 tablespoon olive oil
Salt
Espelette pepper

Prepare the fennel and apricots
Peel, wash, and dry the fennel bulbs. Rinse, dry, halve, and pit the apricots. Squeeze the oranges. Chop the coriander seeds.

Heat the olive oil in a cast-iron pan. Season the fennel bulbs with salt and brown lightly on all sides. Add the chopped coriander seeds, the orange juice, and a pinch of Espelette pepper.

Cook for 8 minutes over medium heat, turning the fennel over from time to time. Add the apricot halves and continue to cook over medium heat for 5 minutes.

Finish and serve
Check and adjust the seasoning. Transfer the fennel and apricots to a serving dish or arrange on individual plates. Reduce the cooking liquid a little if it is too thin and pour over the dish.

AD - If you can't find baby fennel bulbs, take 2 large bulbs and quarter them vertically.

PN - This is a very good recipe if you want to prepare your skin for a tan: it gives you a shot of carotenoids, since fennel and apricots have these in abundance.

SCARPACCIA (ZUCCHINI PIE)

SERVES 4
PREPARATION TIME: 20 MINUTES
REST TIME: 30 MINUTES
COOK TIME: 15 MINUTES

500 grams - 1 pound 2 ounces
small zucchini (courgettes)
Salt
5 Welsh onions or scallions
2 cloves garlic
2 eggs
4 heaping tablespoons
chickpea flour
5 tablespoons grated Parmesan
cheese
100 milliliters - 1/3 cup
plus 1 tablespoon lowfat (2%)
milk
Freshly ground pepper
Olive oil

Prepare the vegetables
Wash and dry the zucchini and trim the ends. Cut them into small dice. Put them in a bowl, season with salt, and leave for 30 minutes to release their residual water. Drain the zucchini over a colander and return them to the bowl.

Wash and dry the onions, remove the outer layer of skin, and cut off the tough tops of the leaves. Mince the rest and add to the bowl with the drained zucchini. Peel and very finely slice the garlic cloves and add them to the bowl.

Make the batter
Break the eggs into a deep earthenware bowl. Add the flour, grated Parmesan, milk, and 100 milliliters - 1/3 cup plus 1 tablespoon water. Whisk to a smooth batter. Add the zucchini, onions, and garlic to the batter and mix. Season with salt and pepper.

Cook the pie
Heat the oven to 210°C - 410°F (gas mark 6). Use a brush to grease a shallow baking pan with olive oil. Pour in the batter and spread it out evenly to a thickness of 3 millimeters - 1/8 inch. Smooth the top. Bake until the pie is golden on the outside and soft on the inside, about 15 minutes.

Finish and serve
Take the pie out of the oven. Let cool, then turn it out of the pan onto a serving dish.

AD - If there are flowers on the ends of your zucchini, don't discard them. Remove their pistils, cut them up coarsely with a pair of scissors, and arrange them over the pie just before serving.

PN - You can also add minced parsley, which is an easy way to boost the amount of vitamin C: Zucchini doesn't have that much of it.

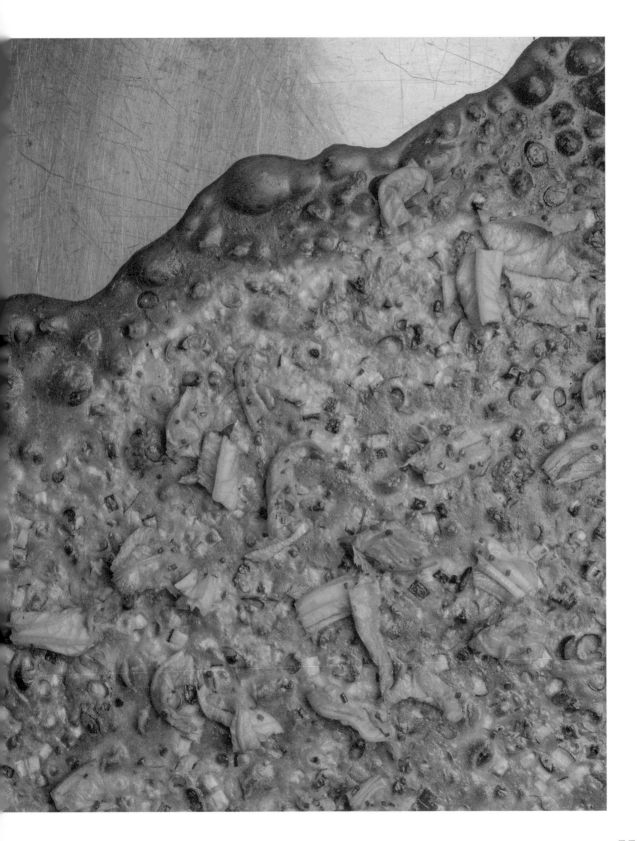

SUMMER VEGETABLE AND FRUIT TARTARE

SERVES 4
PREPARATION TIME: 20 MINUTES
CHILL TIME: 1 HOUR

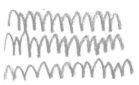

4 large tomatoes
2 peaches, somewhat ripe
1 red bell pepper
1 cucumber
4 Welsh onions or scallions
1/2 white onion
1/2 bunch small-leaf basil
2 tablespoons pine nuts
2 teaspoons sumac
4 tablespoons olive oil
Salt
Freshly ground pepper

AD - Sumac is a spice made from the dried berries of the sumac bush that grows in the Middle East, Sicily, and southern Italy. It has a slightly sour taste and adds sharpness to dishes, so acids such as lemon juice or vinegar are not needed.

PN - Salt should only be added at the end, after tasting. The dish has so many different flavors that very little is needed. You can even do without it, which isn't a bad thing.

Prepare the tomatoes and peaches
Wash and dry the tomatoes. Quarter them and remove the seeds. Dice them. Immerse the peaches in boiling water for 2 minutes, and then shock in ice water. Drain, dry, and peel them, then halve and pit them. Dice the flesh and combine the tomatoes and peaches in a bowl.

Prepare the other vegetables
Wash, dry, and peel the pepper with a vegetable peeler. Halve it, remove the seeds and ribs, then cut each half into a small dice. Wash, dry, and and peel the cucumber. Halve lengthwise, remove the seeds with a spoon, and cut into a small dice. Remove the outer layer of skin from the Welsh onions. Cut off the tough leaves, and cut the remainder into small diagonal slices. Add everything to the bowl with the tomatoes and peaches. Wash, dry, and pluck the basil leaves. Mince half of the leaves and add to the bowl. Set aside the remainder.

Toast the pine nuts
Heat a nonstick frying pan, add the pine nuts, and brown lightly while stirring. Transfer to paper towels.

Finish making the tartare
Add the pine nuts to the bowl with the other ingredients and mix. Season with the sumac and drizzle with the olive oil. Mix again. Check and adjust the seasoning with salt and pepper. Refrigerate the tartare for at least 1 hour before serving.

Serve
Spoon the tartare onto individual plates or into bowls and sprinkle a few of the reserved basil leaves over each.

STUFFED TOMATOES WITH HORSERADISH

100 grams - 3 1/2 ounces/2/3
cup quinoa
8 medium tomatoes
1/2 bunch flat-leaf parsley
1/4 bunch mint
1/4 bunch tarragon
150 grams - 5 1/2 ounces
leftover pot-au-feu vegetables
(see p. 150)
2 onions
1 clove garlic
1 tablespoon olive oil
1 bay leaf
200 grams - 7 ounces leftover
pot-au-feu meat (see p. 150)
2 eggs
5-centimeter- - 2-inch-length
horseradish
Salt

AD - Pot-au-feu doesn't have to be a winter dish. It can also be a summer treat. However, you can't make stuffed tomatoes in winter.

PN - Stuffed tomatoes aren't bad at all, chef. They're well balanced in carbohydrate and protein, with very little fat. I like them a lot, and they make a great one-dish meal.

Cook the quinoa
Rinse the quinoa, put it in a saucepan, and add twice its volume of water. Bring to a boil, lower the heat, cover with a lid, and cook until the water is absorbed, 10–15 minutes. Keep the pan covered and let the quinoa swell up for 10 minutes.

Prepare the tomatoes
In the meantime, wash and dry the tomatoes. Cut off the tops, which will serve as caps. Use a teaspoon to hollow out the tomatoes. Set aside the flesh.

Prepare the herbs and vegetables
Rinse, dry, pluck, and chop the parsley, mint, and tarragon leaves. Cut the pot-au-feu vegetables into a small dice. Peel and chop the onions and garlic.

Make the stuffing
Heat the olive oil in a sauté pan and gently sweat the onions and garlic. Add the tomato flesh and bay leaf, then reduce for 10 minutes. Transfer to a bowl and discard the bay leaf. Shred the pot-au-feu meat, add it to the bowl, and mix. Add the quinoa, diced pot-au-feu vegetables, chopped herbs, and the eggs. Mix. Peel, grate, and add the horseradish. Check and adjust the seasoning with salt.

Assemble and cook the stuffed tomatoes
Heat the oven to 160°C - 325°F (gas mark 3). Fill each tomato with stuffing. As they are filled, put in a baking dish and replace their caps. Bake in the oven for 1 hour 15 minutes. Every 15 minutes baste the tomatoes with their cooking liquid.

GRILLED VEGETABLE TERRINE

SERVES 4-6
PREPARATION TIME: 25 MINUTES
COOK TIME: 10 MINUTES
REST TIME: 8 HOURS

1 red bell pepper
1 yellow bell pepper
1 eggplant (aubergine)
2 zucchini (courgettes)
2 red onions
1/2 bunch flat-leaf parsley
1/2 bunch cilantro (coriander)
1/2 bunch basil
Salt
5 tablespoon olive oil
3 pinches Espelette pepper
4 sprigs thyme
150 grams - 5 1/2 ounces tomato confit petals

AD - The quintessential summer dish. It takes a little while to prepare, but you can make it in advance. The terrine will keep very well in the refrigerator for at least 24 hours.

PN - Serve this terrine as a snack or an appetizer with slices of whole-wheat toast. Or serve it as a main with a cold meat or ham. Finish with a cheese and fruit, and there you have a complete family meal.

Prepare the vegetables and herbs several hours ahead
Use a mandoline with safety guard to slice the peppers, eggplant, and zucchini into 1-centimeter- - 1/2-inch-thick slices. Peel the onions and slice them the same way.

Rinse, dry, and pluck the parsley, cilantro, and basil leaves. Coarsely chop the herbs and put them in a bowl.

Grill the vegetables
Heat a grill pan or flat top grill. Season the vegetable slices with salt and grill for 1 minute on each side, in batches if necessary. Transfer each batch to a large dish.

When all of the vegetables have been grilled, drizzle them with the olive oil, sprinkle with the Espelette pepper, and add the chopped herbs. Pluck the thyme and add the leaves. Toss together with your hands.

Make the terrine
Line a 22-centimeter- - 8 3/4-inch-square terrine mold with a large sheet of plastic wrap (cling film), leaving a good margin over the edges of the mold. Place the vegetable slices in successive layers, alternating from time to time with the tomato confit petals. Press well with the back of the spoon.

Cover with the plastic wrap, and then with a piece of cardboard the size of the mold. Place a weight on the top. Refrigerate for at least 8 hours.

Finish and serve
Remove the weight and turn the terrine out onto a dish. Slice and serve.

TOMATOES

Having always grown wild in South America and later domesticated, the tomato was discovered in Peru by the Spanish conquistadors in the fifteenth century. It soon arrived in Europe, but was feared because it was thought to be poisonous. However, the people of Provence began to grow it in the seventeenth century and a group of them introduced it to Paris on July 14, 1790, to celebrate the anniversary of the fall of the Bastille. As nobody was poisoned by eating it, the market gardeners of Paris planted tomato seeds, and its cultivation expanded throughout France and Europe. The tomato is a fruit, as everybody knows, but it is the most widely used vegetable. During the twentieth century, it underwent a great deal of mutations and was genetically manipulated to produce a perfect, highly marketable shape, to grow year-round, and to withstand rough treatment when shipped. The result was an odorless and tasteless fruit. Fortunately, farmers have taken to reviving heirloom varieties with different shapes, sizes, flavors, and colors.

● VARIETIES AND SEASONS

Tomatoes are classified by their color: reds and pinks, oranges and yellows, pepper-shaped, multicolored, and green, black, and white. They are also classified by their shape and size: round, ribbed (among them the beefsteak tomato has been "industrialized"), elongated, and small (cherry tomato). Depending on the variety, tomatoes are on the market from May through September.

● CHOOSING AND STORAGE

Good tomatoes should be purchased at a market, from small farmers who grow them in open fields, and, wherever possible, organically. And they should only be bought in season. They should be stored at room temperature in a cool place-the refrigerator causes their flavor and texture to deteriorate.

● NUTRITION

While low in calories, tomatoes are rich in many protective antioxidants, such as carotenoids, vitamin C, vitamin E, polyphenols, and lycopene. The action of the lycophene is enhanced when the tomatoes are cooked.

● USES AND COMBINATIONS

Whether raw or cooked, savory or sweet, tomatoes are suited to numerous cold and hot preparations. They go well with practically everything: spices, condiments, other vegetables, fruits, cereals, meats, and fish.

PROVENÇAL TOMATOES

SERVES 4
PREPARATION TIME: 15 MINUTES
COOK TIME: 50 MINUTES

Salt
150 grams - 3/4 cup plus 2
tablespoons kasha
6 heirloom tomatoes
Freshly ground pepper
3 cloves garlic
1/2 bunch flat-leaf parsley
Store-bought bread crumbs
Olive oil

Prepare the kasha
Bring lightly salted water to a boil in a saucepan. Add the kasha. Blanch for 3 minutes and then drain.

Prepare the tomatoes
Wash, dry, and halve the tomatoes. Squeeze lightly to remove their water and seeds. Lay side by side in a gratin dish and season with salt and pepper.

Peel the garlic cloves, remove the green core (germ), chop the garlic, and put in a bowl. Rinse, dry, pluck, and chop the parsley leaves. Add to the bowl with the garlic along with the blanched kasha and mix. Spread the mixture over the tomatoes and sprinkle with the bread crumbs.

Cook and serve the tomatoes
Heat the oven to 170°C - 340°F (gas mark 3-4). Drizzle the gratin dish generously with olive oil and put it in the oven for 45 minutes. Serve immediately in the gratin dish or plate individually.

AD - Kasha is toasted buckwheat groats with a very pleasant, slightly smoky flavor. It is common in Russian and Polish cuisines, often served as a porridge.

PN - Your tomatoes are still Provençal, chef, despite the kasha you've added to them. It's a reference to the Russians who emigrated to the French Riviera during the Russian Revolution of 1917. I think it's great that you've added these slow carbs.

EGGPLANT AND CHOCOLATE

SERVES 4
PREPARATION TIME: 1 HOUR
COOK TIME: 1 HOUR 15 MINUTES
CHILL TIME: 4 HOURS

1 (250-gram - 9-ounce)
eggplant
160 grams - 5 3/4 ounces
dark chocolate (70 percent
cocoa)
150 milliliters - 2/3 cup
lowfat (2%) milk
150 grams - 2/3 cup crème
fraîche
3 egg yolks
30 grams - 1 ounce/2 1/2
tablespoons superfine (caster)
sugar

AD - It's amazing how Christophe Saintagne's creativity has brought about this marriage between eggplant and chocolate. They go so well together. We really should think about using vegetables in desserts more often.

PN - I like that idea, too. It's mouth-watering. What's more, this dessert isn't really sweet, which is great.

Prepare the eggplant

Heat the oven to 180°C - 350°F (gas mark 4). Wash, dry, and halve the eggplant lengthwise. Score the flesh with the tip of a knife. Put the eggplant halves on a baking sheet and cook in the oven for 1 hour.

Make the chocolate crémeux

Grate the chocolate (or break into very small pieces) and put in a bowl. Heat the milk and crème fraîche in a saucepan over medium heat; bring to a boil.

In the meantime, beat the egg yolks and sugar together until the mixture turns pale. Gradually whisk the boiling milk and cream into the egg yolks and sugar. Immediately return the mixture to the saucepan. Cook over low heat while stirring constantly until the mixture is thick enough to coat a spoon, like a crème anglaise. Pour one third of this custard over the chocolate and mix until it is well melted; continue adding the custard in thirds and mixing. Set aside.

Finish the eggplant

Take the eggplant halves out of the oven and let cool. Use a teaspoon to scoop out their flesh; transfer it to a bowl. Mush well with a fork and mix until smooth.

Finish the dessert

Add the cold eggplant puree to the bowl with the chocolate crémeux. Stir until smooth. Spread the mixture evenly in a porcelain bowl. Refrigerate for at least 4 hours.

Serve

Put the bowl on the table. Guests can make their own quenelles of the dessert, or serve quenelles on individual chilled plates.

CHERRY AND ALMOND CLAFOUTIS

SERVES 4
PREPARATION TIME: 15 MINUTES
COOK TIME: 35 MINUTES

2 (110-gram - 4-ounce) eggs
80 grams - 2 3/4 ounces/1
cup plus 1 tablespoon
superfine (caster) sugar
1 gram - 2 3/4 pinches salt
200 grams - 7 ounces/2 cups
almond meal (ground almonds)
30 grams - 1 ounce/1/4 cup
flour
100 grams - 3 1/2 ounces/1/3
cup plus 2 tablespoons crème
fraîche
30 large cherries
10 grams - 3/8 ounce/2
teaspoons butter
2 tablespoons sliced (flaked)
almonds
Confectioners' (icing) sugar
for dusting

Make the clafoutis batter
Break the eggs into a mixing bowl and whisk with them with the sugar. When well mixed, add the salt and almond meal, then the flour, and finally the crème fraîche, mixing well with each addition. Set aside in the refrigerator.

Prepare the cherries
Wash, dry, hull, and pit the cherries.

Assemble and bake the clafoutis
Heat the oven to 170°C - 340°F (gas mark 3–4). Grease a 22-centimeter- - 8 3/4-inch-diameter porcelain tart pan with the butter and fill it with the clafoutis batter. Cover with the cherries, pressing them into the batter. Sprinkle with the sliced almonds.

Place the pan on a baking sheet and bake for 35 minutes. Check that it is cooked by inserting the tip of a knife into the clafoutis. The batter should have coagulated and the knife should come out clean.

Remove the clafoutis from the oven and sprinkle with confectioners' (icing) sugar. Serve hot or cold in the mold.

AD - The cherries have to be very ripe. Choose very large ones; they're easier to pit. Do it over a bowl so that you don't waste the juice that's bound to come out.

PN - Preferably a light, mostly vegetarian meal before trying this clafoutis, otherwise you won't be hungry enough to take full advantage of it.

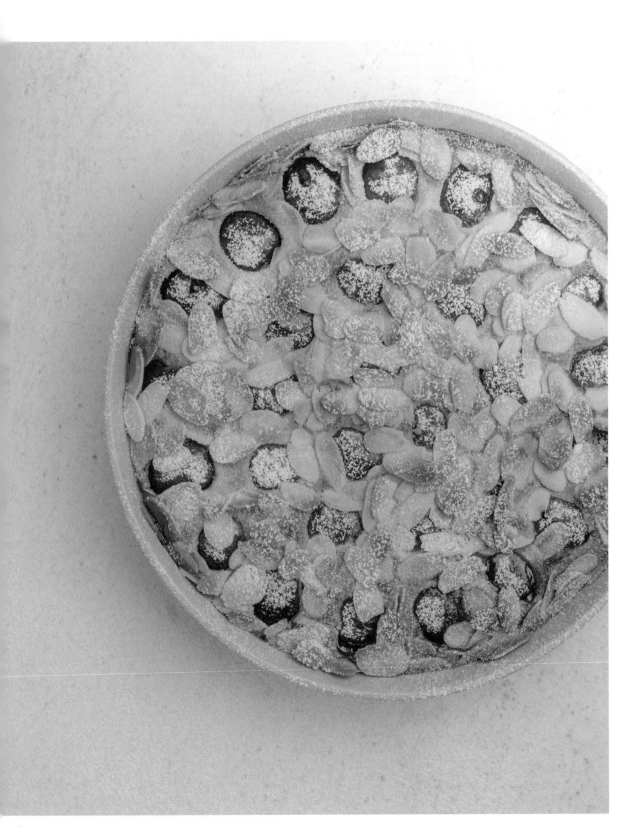

GLUTEN-FREE RASPBERRY FINANCIERS

MAKES 8 FINANCIERS
PREPARATION TIME: 15 MINUTES
REST TIME: 15 MINUTES
COOK TIME: 10 MINUTES

100 grams - 3 1/2 ounces/1/3 cup plus 1 tablespoon egg whites (3-4 whites)
100 grams - 3 1/2 ounces/7 tablespoons butter, plus more for greasing
55 grams - 2 ounces/1/2 cup almond meal (ground almonds)
100 grams - 3 1/2 ounces/3/4 cup confectioners' (icing) sugar
35 grams - 1 ounce/1/3 cup chickpea flour plus more for the molds
1 vanilla bean (pod)
16 large raspberries
20 grams - 3/4 ounce/ 3 tablespoons sliced (flaked) almonds

AD - Remember not to discard the vanilla bean after scraping out the seeds. It still has a lot of flavor and can be used for flavoring milk or cream. As for the remaining egg yolks, use one to make an eggplant mayonnaise (see p. 284) and the others for a crème anglaise.

PN - These are financiers that gluten-free people will absolutely love. Crème anglaise and a serving of fresh raspberries make a good accompaniment for these financiers.

Prepare the egg whites and butter
Separate the eggs 10–15 minutes before using them to let the whites come to room temperature. Cut the butter into pieces and melt in a saucepan over medium heat until it has a brown color (a *beurre noisette* – brown butter with a light hazelnut flavor). Remove from the heat.

Make the financier batter
Combine the almond meal, confectioners' sugar, and chickpea flour in a mixing bowl. Split open the vanilla bean, scrape out the seeds into the bowl, and mix. Add the egg whites and mix again. Add the warm beurre noisette and mix well.

Assemble and bake the financiers
Heat the oven to 200°C - 400°F (gas mark 6). Grease eight 4.5-centimeter- - 1 3/4-inch-diameter half-sphere molds with butter and flour. Fill the molds halfway with the batter and put 2 raspberries in each. Finish filling with the batter, making sure to cover the raspberries. Sprinkle with sliced almonds. Place the molds on a tray and bake the financiers for 6–8 minutes.

Finish
Remove the tray from the oven and transfer the molds to a wire rack. Let cool, then unmold. Serve warm or cold.

RED BELL PEPPER SORBET, TOMATO CONFIT, AND ESPELETTE PEPPER

SERVES 4
PREPARATION TIME: 20 MINUTES
COOK TIME: 15 MINUTES
REST TIME: 3 HOURS

7 red bell peppers, about 800
grams - 1 pound 12 ounces
100 milliliters - 1/3 cup
plus 1 tablespoon water
150 grams - 2/3 cup light
(single) cream
1 tablespoon honey
4 grams - 2 teaspoons
Espelette pepper, plus more
for dusting
1 loaf rye bread
1 (250-gram - 9-ounce)
container *faisselle* cheese
(Cottage cheese)
2 sprigs basil
16 petals tomato confit (see
p. 363)
Olive oil for drizzling

AD - This red bell pepper sorbet is nothing like what you'd expect. You're sure to surprise your guests with this dessert. The peppers have to be very ripe.

PN - A dessert made with vegetables and fromage frais is something I adore. With vitamins, minerals, dietary fiber, and calcium, it's fantastic. And it's barely even sweet.

Make the bell pepper juice for the sorbet
Peel the peppers with a vegetable peeler. Cut them open and remove the seeds and ribs. Cut into pieces and pass through a juicer or blend to a puree and filter the juice through a conical strainer.

Make the red bell pepper sorbet
Combine the water, cream, honey, and Espelette pepper in a saucepan and heat very gently to 50°C - 120°F, stirring from time to time. Blend with a handheld immersion blender and add to the bell pepper juice. Blend briefly again. Let the mixture sit at room temperature for at least 3 hours. Blend again, then transfer to an ice cream maker and churn to a sorbet.

Dry out the bread
Heat the oven to 120°C - 250°F (gas mark 2). Cut four slices from the bread that are about 3 millimeters - 1/8 inch thick. Put them on a baking sheet and into the oven until they are dried out, about 15 minutes.

Prepare the cream cheese and basil
Drain the faisselle cheese in a strainer. Rinse, dry, pluck, and mince the basil leaves.

Finish
Arrange a quarter of the cheese, 1 quenelle of sorbet, 4 tomato confit petals, and a little basil on each of four chilled plates. Add a slice of dried bread, drizzle with a little olive oil, and sprinkle with Espelette pepper.

GARLIC CONFIT

MAKES 1 JAR
PREPARATION TIME: 5 MINUTES
COOK TIME: 1 HOUR

3 heads pink or new garlic
2 sprigs thyme
1 sprig rosemary
15 black peppercorns
1 pinch coarse salt
Olive oil

Clean the jar
Bring water to a boil in a large cast-iron pot or a stock-pot. Put the jar and the lid in the pot and boil for 10 minutes. Put them upside down on a clean cloth and let it cool.

Prepare the garlic cloves
Divide the heads of garlic into individual cloves. Separate out the smallest cloves and only keep the largest ones. Do not peel them, but remove any excess skin that comes off easily.

Make the garlic confit
Put the garlic cloves in a saucepan. Add the thyme, rosemary, peppercorns, and salt. Cover the cloves with olive oil. Place the pan over low heat. The oil has to reach a temperature of about 70°C - 160°F, but do not let it boil. Cook for 45 minutes–1 hour, monitoring the temperature.

Prepare the jar
Remove the pan from the heat and let the garlic cool. Use a skimmer to remove the garlic cloves from the oil and transfer them to the dry jar. Tap the jar to compact the cloves, then pour the cooking oil over them. Close the jar tightly and store in the refrigerator for 2-3 months.

AD – This garlic confit is used in all kinds of ways: for flavoring vegetables, sauces, salads. It immediately elevates them. Once you've used up the garlic, the remaining flavored oil can be used for salads or sautéing potatoes.

PN – Store the garlic in the darkness of the refrigerator, because light makes fatty acids in the oil turn rancid. Use it generously, because garlic is a truly natural health food.

PRESERVED EGGPLANTS

MAKES ENOUGH TO FILL ONE 2-LITER -
67.6-FLUID-OUNCE JAR
PREPARATION TIME: 30 MINUTES
STERILIZATION TIME: 10 MINUTES + 1 HOUR
REST TIME: 1 HOUR

2 kilograms - 4 pounds 8
ounces medium eggplants
Olive oil
Salt
1 small bird's-eye chili
pepper
1 bay leaf
1 sprig thyme
1 sprig rosemary
2 cloves garlic
1.5 liters - 6 1/3 cups
olive oil

Clean the jar
Bring water to a boil in a large cast-iron pot or a stock-pot. Put the jar and the lid in the pot and boil for 10 minutes. Put them upside down on a clean cloth and let it cool.

Prepare the eggplants
Wash, dry, and cut the eggplants into 2-centimeter- - 3/4-inch-thick slices. Heat a grill pan and grease it with a little olive oil. Grill the eggplant slices for 1 minute on each side. As they are done, transfer to a wire rack or a dish. Season with salt.

Prepare the jar
Put the eggplant slices in the dry jar. Add the chili pepper, bay leaf, thyme, and rosemary. Crush the garlic cloves and add them to the jar. Then pour the oil into the jar to completely cover the eggplants.

Close the jar. Put it in a large cast-iron pot and cover with water. Boil the jar in the water for 1 hour.

Turn off the heat and let the jar cool in the water for the same length of time. Then store in the pantry for few months. Once opened, you need to store it in the fridge for few days only

AD - You can use these eggplants as a condiment during the following winter, with pasta, rice, or another grain, or spread over bread.

PN - When you open the jar, you have to store it in the refrigerator, like other bottled preserves. Once opened, you can keep them few days only. I'm going to make it in small jars, chef, because they'll be easier to manage.

TOMATO COULIS

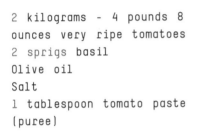

MAKES ENOUGH TO FILL ONE
500-MILLILITER - 16.9-FLUID-OUNCE JAR
PREPARATION TIME: 35 MINUTES
COOK TIME: 50 MINUTES
STERILIZATION TIME: 10 MINUTES PLUS 45 MINUTES
REST TIME: 45 MINUTES

2 kilograms - 4 pounds 8 ounces very ripe tomatoes
2 sprigs basil
Olive oil
Salt
1 tablespoon tomato paste (puree)

Clean the jar
Bring water to a boil in a large cast-iron pot or a stock-pot. Put the jar and the lid in the pot and boil for 10 minutes. Put them upside down on a clean cloth and let it cool.

Prepare the tomatoes
Wash and dry the tomatoes and remove their stems. Cut a cross-like incision on the base. Squeeze them over a bowl to remove the seeds.

Put the deseeded tomatoes in another bowl. Put a strainer over the bowl with the deseeded tomatoes and filter the collected juice and seeds into it. Press with the back of a spoon to extract as much juice as possible. Rinse, dry, pluck, and coarsely chop the basil leaves. Heat a little olive oil in a cast-iron pan and add the tomatoes. Stir, season with salt, and add the basil and tomato paste. Cook for about 50 minutes over medium heat, stirring from time to time.

Prepare the jar
Remove the pan from the heat and transfer its contents to a blender. Blend until smooth. You can also blend the contents of the pan with a handheld immersion blender.

Pour this coulis into the dry jar. Close the lid and put it in a cast-iron pot. Cover with water and boil for 45 minutes. Let cool inside the water and then store in a pantry for few months. Once opened, you need to store it in the fridge for few days only.

AD – Don't add onion, garlic, thyme, or other aromatics to the coulis, as these will give it a bad taste while it is stored. It is simple enough to add them when you use it.

PN – Use old tomatoes to make this coulis. Recover the seeds, dry them, and keep them to plant in your garden the following spring. If you don't have a garden, plant them in pots on your balcony or windowsill.

FI GS

Native to Central Asia, the fig tree spread to the Mediterranean region, where it has become emblematic. But it also grows well in other regions. This tree obviously produces the fig, which is known by the term fruit while actually not being one. It is actually the fig tree's floral receptacle, or inflorescence, known as the synconium, which is picked when mature. By that stage, the fig has the shape of a small, more or less rounded pear, which is covered by a thick skin that protects a pinkish red flesh filled with tiny seeds. There are more than 150 varieties of fig trees, which are grown in different hot countries. Most figs are dried after picking. While this was once done under the sun, it is now carried out in convection ovens, after which the figs are washed in salted water and commonly treated with sulfites, the source of some allergies.

VARIETIES AND SEASONS
There are three main types of figs, classified by color. Certain trees produce two crops a year, at the end of spring and in the fall; others only produce one crop, picked at the end of summer. Traditionally, fig season runs June through December. Favorite purple figs include the well-known Black Mission, the popular Brown Turkey, and King. Calimyrna, Sierra, and Kadota figs are the most popular green fig varieties.

CHOOSING AND STORAGE
A fig at peak ripeness has a "tear in its eye," a drop of syrup that comes through the orifice at the base of the fruit. It may also be slightly wrinkled. A hard, smooth, and firm fig is not good. Fresh figs are stored at room temperature, but for only a very short time because they start to ferment quickly. Do not refrigerate them. Dried figs should be stored in a dry place in an airtight container.

NUTRITION
Figs are high in carbohydrate, dietary fiber, minerals, and antioxidants (particularly purple figs). Dried figs bring together all of these benefits.

USES AND COMBINATIONS
Fresh figs should never be washed or peeled, only dried, and they can be roasted, poached, and candied. Raw figs combine well with Parma ham or another type of cured ham, and with cheese. Dried figs are used in breads, cakes, tagines, and pastilla, and with foie gras. They are rehydrated to make compotes.

PRESERVED FRUIT TO GET THROUGH THE WINTER

MAKES ENOUGH TO FILL ONE 1-LITER -
33.8-FLUID-OUNCE JAR PER FRUIT
PREPARATION TIME: 20 MINUTES
STERILIZATION TIME: 25-40 MINUTES
REST TIME: 25-40 MINUTES

FOR THE APRICOTS
20 apricots
1 vanilla bean
10 black peppercorns
250 grams - 2 ounces/1 1/3
cups rapadura sugar

FOR THE FIGS
20 figs
3 grams - 1 1/2 teaspoons
quatre épices spice mix
10 black peppercorns
100 grams - 3 1/2 ounces/1/2
cup rapadura sugar

FOR THE PLUMS
20 quetsch plums or any other
plums
1 vanilla bean
10 black peppercorns
200 milliliters - 3/4 cup
plus 1 tablespoon plum brandy
100 grams - 3 1/2 ounces/1/2
cup rapadura sugar

AD - The fruits have to be very ripe.
There's no point preserving half-ripe
fruits; sterilization won't improve them.
Purchase good organic fruits. And make
several jars; it really doesn't take
long.

PN - Naturally you won't be preserving the fruit in syrup filled with
pesticides. These fruits will be welcome
during the winter to give variety to
your desserts. They're fantastic with
fromage blanc.

Clean the jars
Bring water to a boil in a large cast-iron pot or a stock-pot. Put the jars and the lids in the pot and boil for 10 minutes. Put them upside down on a clean cloth and let it cool.

Make the apricot jar
Wash, dry, halve, and pit the apricots. Pack them well into one of the dry jars. Split the vanilla bean, scrape out the seeds, and add the bean and seeds to the jar.

Make the fig jar
Wash and dry the figs and put them in one of the dry jars. Add the spice mix and peppercorns.

Make the plum jar
Wash, dry, halve, and pit the plums and put them in the remaining dry jar. Cut the vanilla bean in half and add to the jar, together with the peppercorns, followed by the plum brandy.

Cook the syrup for all jars
For each fruit, combine 1 liter - 4 1/4 cups water and the specified amount of rapadura sugar for the fruit in a saucepan and bring to a boil.

Finish preparing each jar
Cover the fruits with the boiling syrup. Close each jar tightly. Put the jars in separate large cast-iron pot and cover with water (5 centimeters - 2 inches above the lid). Cover the pot with its lid and boil the figs for 25 minutes, the plums for 30 minutes, and the apricots for 40 minutes. Let the jars cool in the water. Store in a pantry for few months. Once opened, you need to store it in the fridge for few days only

359

PICKLED HOT PEPPERS

MAKES ENOUGH TO FILL ONE 2-LITER - 67.6-FLUID-OUNCE JAR

PREPARATION TIME: 5 MINUTES

COOK TIME: 2 MINUTES

PICKLING TIME: 2 MONTHS

20 cayenne peppers
1-5 cloves garlic, according to taste
1 sprig fresh thyme, plus a few thyme leaves
1 sprig fresh marjoram
1 teaspoon peppercorns
1.5 liters - 3 1/3 cups wine vinegar

Prepare the jar and peppers

Bring water to a boil in a large cast-iron pot or a stock-pot. Put the jar and the lid in the pot and boil for 10 minutes. Put them upside down on a clean cloth and let it cool.

Wash the peppers and split each one along their length to remove all the seeds. Peel the garlic cloves and remove the green cores (germs). Put the peppers, garlic, thyme sprig and leaves, marjoram, and peppercorns in the jar.

Prepare the liquid and finish the jars

Bring the vinegar to a boil in a saucepan. Pour the boiling liquid into the jar over the peppers, making sure they are well covered. Close the jar, turn it upside down on a clean cloth, and let cool. Store them in a pantry and let the peppers pickle for 2 months before use.

AD - Wear disposable gloves when preparing the peppers, otherwise you risk having your hands attacked by capsaicin, the compound that gives peppers their bite. Be careful with your eyes, too.

PN - Capsaicin is an active alkaloid that is found to a greater or lesser degree in all chili peppers and gives them their heat. Its strength is classified according to the Scoville scale. Bell peppers have the lowest score (0 out of 10), while Cayenne peppers score an 8.

TOMATO CONFIT

MAKES ABOUT 300 GRAMS
- 10.5 OUNCES
PREPARATION TIME: 20 MINUTES
REST TIME: 2-3 HOURS

1 kilogram - 2 pounds 4 ounces very ripe tomatoes
1 clove garlic
Olive oil
Salt
3 sprigs thyme

Prepare the tomatoes and garlic
Peel the tomatoes using a tomato peeler. Halve them and remove the seeds. Peel the garlic clove.

Prepare and cook the tomato confit
Heat the oven to 100°C - 210°F (gas mark 4).
Put the tomatoes in a bowl. Drizzle with 4 tablespoons olive oil and season lightly with salt. Mix carefully to coat and season the tomatoes well.

Rub the inside of a shallow baking pan with the garlic clove. Pluck the thyme over the pan, then spread the tomato halves out, spacing them apart so that they do not touch. Scrape the rest of the liquid from the bowl using a flexible spatula (scraper) so that nothing is wasted. Pour it over the tomatoes.

Slide the pan into the oven and leave the door ajar to allow a little stream of air to enter. Cook for 2-3 hours, watching them carefully and turning the drier tomato halves rounded side down and the more moist ones rounded side up.

If there are halves (petals) that cook faster, remove them and transfer to a plate. They need to be dry outside but still soft inside.

Finish
When they are all done, take the pan out of the oven and let the tomato petals cool. Put them in an airtight container or jar and cover with olive oil. Seal the container or jar and store in the refrigerator.

AD - Tomatoes are traditionally peeled by soaking them in boiling water to remove their skin more easily. But it is much faster if you use a tomato peeler.

PN - The more you cook a tomato, the more its lycopene, the main antioxidant it contains, is active. These tomatoes are perfect in this respect.

APPENDIX

RAVIOLI DOUGH

MAKES 250 GRAMS - 9 OUNCES /
1 1/2 CUPS DOUGH

250 grams - 9 ounces/1 1/2 cups
type 45 flour
3 eggs
2 tablespoons olive oil
Salt

Combine the flour, eggs, olive oil, and a
pinch of salt in a bowl. Mix the ingredients
together with your fingers, then knead until
the dough is smooth. Roll into a ball, cover
with plastic wrap (cling film), and refrigerate
for at least 3 hours.

BURGER BUNS

FOR 4 BURGER BUNS

50 grams - 2 ounces/2 tablespoons
butter, plus more for greasing
160 milliliters - 2/3 cup plus 2
teaspoons lowfat (2%) milk
5 grams - 1/6 ounce active dry yeast
250 grams - 9 ounces/2 cups flour
5 grams - scant 1 teaspoon salt
5 grams - 1 teaspoon sugar
2 egg yolks
Flaxseeds, sunflower seeds, sesame
seeds

Take the butter out of the refrigerator, cut
it into small pieces, and let soften. Warm
150 milliliters - 2/3 cup milk. Put the yeast
in a bowl and dissolve with the warm milk.
Mix the flour, salt, and sugar together in the
bowl of a stand mixer fitted with the dough
hook, then add the yeast and milk mixture.
When the ingredients are all well mixed, add
1 egg yolk and the softened butter. Knead
for 8–10 minutes. Put the dough in a bowl
and cut it into four 60-gram - 2 1/8-ounce
pieces. Roll them into balls between your
palms. Grease a baking sheet with butter
and lay the balls on it.
Mix the remaining egg yolk with the
remaining milk (10 milliliters - 2 teaspoons).
Use a brush to glaze the tops of the buns
(so that they rise well). Sprinkle each bun
with seeds. Cover the baking sheet with
a clean kitchen cloth and rest at room
temperature for 1 hour.
Heat the oven to 180°C - 350°F (gas mark
4) and bake the buns for 12–15 minutes.
Take them out, transfer them to a wire rack,
and let cool.

BASIC PASTRY

MAKES 275 GRAMS - 9 OUNCES /
2/3 CUPS PASTRY

200 grams - 7 ounces/1 1/3 cups
flour
50 grams - 1/3 cup potato starch
20 grams - 3/8 ounce/2 teaspoons
butter
5 grams - scant 1 teaspoon salt
1 egg

Combine the flour, starch, butter in small pieces, and salt in the bowl of a stand mixer fitted with the paddle. Mix for 10 seconds on medium speed to form a coarse mixture. Add the egg and 50 milliliters - 2 1/2 tablespoons water, mix again, and stop the mixer when the dough has taken shape. Transfer to a bowl, cover with plastic wrap (cling film), and refrigerate for 1 hour.

PIZZA DOUGH

MAKES 145 GRAMS - 5 1/8 /
1 1/4 CUPS DOUGH

1 teaspoon active dry yeast or 1/4
of a 7-gram - 1/4-ounce envelope
(sachet) dried yeast
145 grams - 5 1/8 ounces/1 1/4 cups
type 45 flour
2 pinches salt
1 teaspoon olive oil

Dissolve the yeast in a little warm water. Combine the flour, salt, olive oil, and 2 tablespoons cold water in the bowl of a stand mixer fitted with a dough hook. Mix on low speed until the dough is smooth. Roll into a ball, cover with a damp cloth, and let rise at room temperature for at least 30 minutes.

TABLE OF RECIPES

FALL

TABLE OF RECIPES

SUMMER

INDEX BY INGREDIENTS

FALL

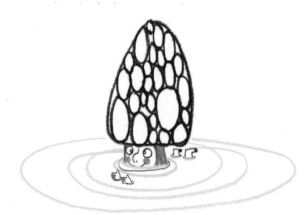

WINTER

INDEX BY PREPARATION TIME

SP RI NG

SU
MM
ER

LESS THAN 15 MINUTES

LESS THAN 30 MINUTES

30 - 45 MINUTES

45 MINUTES - 1 HOUR

1 - 2 HOURS

MORE THAN 2 HOURS

PAULE NEYRAT

The granddaughter of a chef and nutritionist, Paule Neyrat has always combined her work in the fields of nutrition and gastronomy. As the creator of the Escoffier Foundation internship program for perfecting chefs' skills, she has been working with the greatest of them for about twenty years. And as a journalist specializing in food and nutrition, she is also the author of different books mainly published by Alain Ducasse Édition, with whom she is a regular collaborator.

CHRISTOPHE SAINTAGNE

This native of Normandy learned the basics of his profession in Conteville, where he trained under Guillaume Louet at the Auberge du Vieux Logis. He then went to work for Philippe Groult at his Amphyclés restaurant in Paris in 1998. He fulfilled his military service obligations at the Élysée Palace in 1999, before joining Alain Ducasse at 59 Poincaré and later at the Plaza Athénée. In 2002 he was made head chef of the Aux Lyonnais restaurant in Paris. Between 2005 and 2008, he worked with Jean-François Piège at the Hôtel de Crillon as his second in command, before returning to Alain Ducasse in 2009 as executive chef. After running the kitchens at the Plaza Athénée between 2010 and 2013, and the cuisine at the Hôtel Meurice from 2013 to 2015, he is now head of his own restaurant in Paris : Papillon.

ACKNOWLEDGMENTS
Paule Neyrat would like to thank Christophe Saintaigne and Pierre Monetta.
Christophe Saintagne would like to thank Diego Ferrari, Pere Venturos Villalba, Anthony Denon Madinska, Jeremy Bellone, Cédric Grolet, and Yohann Caron for their help during shooting.

COLLECTION DIRECTOR
Alain Ducasse

DIRECTOR
Aurore Charoy

EDITORIAL MANAGER
Alice Gouget

EDITOR
Claire Dupuy

PHOTOGRAPHY
Pierre Monetta

DESIGN
Sarah Bazennerye

ILLUSTRATIONS
Christine Roussey

ART DIRECTION & GRAPHIC DESIGN
Soins Graphiques
Pierre Tachon et Sophie Brice

PHOTOENGRAVING
Nord Compo

PROOFREADING
Karine Elsener

MARKETING & COMMUNICATION
Camille Gonnet

The editor would like to thank Maud Rogers for her invaluable help.

First published in English in 2017
by Rizzoli International Publications, Inc.
300 Park Avenue South
New York, NY 10010
www.rizzoliusa.com

Nature, vol. 2 © 2015 by Alain Ducasse Édition

2017 2018 2019 2020 / 10 9 8 7 6 5 4 3 2 1
Distributed in the U.S. trade by Random House, New York
Printed in China

ISBN-13: 978-0-8478-5875-0
Library of Congress Catalog Control Number: 2016959417

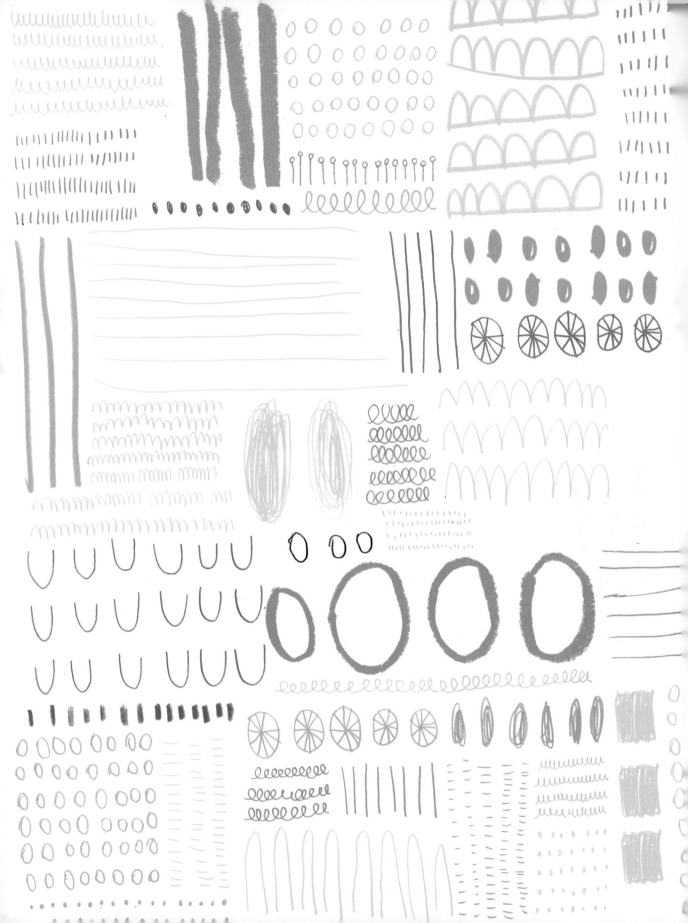